Learn Cybersecurity

Protect Your Digital Assets

SELLAPPAN PALANIAPPAN

RAJASVARAN LOGESWARAN

SUMIT DHARIWAL

Made with ❤on the Notion Press Platform

www.notionpress.com

Preface

Welcome to Learn Cybersecurity: Protect Your Digital Assets, a practical guide to mastering cybersecurity essentials in today's digital landscape.

Each chapter in this book delves into a specific aspect of cybersecurity, providing foundational knowledge, current practices, and actionable insights. To reinforce these concepts, example Python code is provided at the end of each chapter, illustrating some key elements discussed. These code examples offer practical applications, helping readers better understand and implement cybersecurity measures.

We begin with an Introduction to Cybersecurity, covering its importance, evolution, and the CIA Triad—Confidentiality, Integrity, and Availability. Cyber Threats and Attack Vectors explores threats like malware, phishing, and social engineering, along with effective mitigation strategies.

Fundamentals of Network Security introduces key concepts such as network protocols, firewalls, VPNs, and IDS/IPS. Endpoint and Application Security focuses on safeguarding devices and applications using tools like antivirus software, Endpoint Protection Platforms (EPP), and secure coding practices.

Cryptography and Encryption explains symmetric and asymmetric encryption, digital signatures, and Public Key Infrastructure (PKI). Identity and Access Management (IAM) covers essential authentication methods, including passwords, biometrics, and Multi-Factor Authentication (MFA).

Incident Response and Management outlines effective response strategies, while Data Protection and Privacy addresses data handling, encryption, and compliance with laws like GDPR and HIPAA.

Security Awareness and Training emphasizes the importance of educating employees and fostering a proactive security culture. Application Security covers securing the software lifecycle, testing methodologies, and DevSecOps.

Cloud Security addresses the unique challenges of securing cloud environments, while Mobile and IoT Security explores methods for securing connected devices. Advanced Persistent Threats (APTs) examines sophisticated cyberattacks, with strategies for detection and defense.

Blockchain for Security, highlights the more recent potential of blockchain's role in data security and decentralized identity. Emerging Technologies and Future Trends covers the impact of AI, quantum computing, and 5G on cybersecurity.

Finally, Legal and Ethical Considerations in Cybersecurity discusses regulations, ethical hacking, and the legal implications of cyber incidents.

This book equips you with the knowledge to navigate cybersecurity challenges and effectively protect your digital assets.

Acknowledgments

The authors would like to express their grateful thanks to Professors Dr Paul Chan, Dr Andy Liew and Dr Azween Abdullah, Nor Adnan Yahya, Dr Asiah Lokman, Dr Preethi Subramaniam, Dr Munir Kolapo Yahya-Imam and Dr Bùi Ngọc Dũng for their encouragement and support throughout the preparation of this manuscript.

We are very grateful to Ms. Kamalinni Mohan Raj and Ms. Nurul Najihah for their very valuable assistance in checking the manuscript for consistency, formatting, and ensuring the accuracy of page and section numbering, as well as for printing draft copies multiple times.

The authors acknowledge the use of visuals sourced from the Internet in this book and express their appreciation for these contributions.

AI tools, particularly ChatGPT and Claude, have provided tremendous assistance in the preparation of this manuscript – duly acknowledged.

Lastly, and most importantly, the authors thank God for granting the energy, motivation, desire, and guidance to successfully undertake and complete this manuscript.

Prof. Dr. P. Sellappan

Prof. Dr. R. Logeswaran

Asst. Prof. Dr. Sumit Dhariwal

About the Authors

Prof. Dr. Sellappan Palaniappan is a Professor of Information Technology at HELP University, Malaysia. With over 30 years of academic experience, his current research interests are in the application of artificial intelligence and machine learning in diverse domains like cybersecurity, data analytics, healthcare, biotechnology, retail, education, agriculture, logistics, and sustainable development initiatives. He is also interested in quantum physics, DNA, neuroscience, and energy, frequency, and vibration for health and wholeness. He has published more than 100 scholarly research papers and authored several widely-used IT textbooks for college and university students.

Prof. Dr. Rajasvaran Logeswaran is a Professor and Dean of Computing and Digital Technology at HELP University, Malaysia. With over 25 years of academic experience, his research interests are in medical image processing, artificial intelligence, data science and cybersecurity, with over 180 publications in books, peer-reviewed journals and international conference proceedings. He actively serves as a speaker at many international conferences, as well as volunteers as a judge in STEM and innovation competitions for schools at the local and international levels. His latest pursuit is as a cybersecurity trainer.

Dr. Sumit Dhariwal is an Assistant Professor at the Centre for AI, Madhav Institute of Technology & Science (MITS-DU), India. He holds a Ph.D. from Malaysia University of Science and Technology. His research interests include image processing, computer vision, AI/ML, green technology, crop disease detection, cybersecurity, and face detection. He has published over 30 papers in reputable journals and conferences.

Table of Contents

Chapter 1

Introduction to Cybersecurity

Learning Outcomes:

Upon completing this chapter, you will be able to:

- *Define and understand the scope of cybersecurity, its critical role in safeguarding digital assets.*
- *Trace the historical evolution of cybersecurity, identifying key milestones and advancements.*
- *Explore and apply the CIA Triad's principles—Confidentiality, Integrity, and Availability—within cybersecurity* strategies.

1.1 Why Cybersecurity?

Cybersecurity encompasses a broad range of practices, technologies, and processes designed to safeguard systems, networks, programs, and data from cyber threats. It involves proactive measures to prevent attacks, detect threats, and mitigate risks when security incidents occur.

Importance of Cybersecurity

Protects Sensitive Information: Cybersecurity measures are crucial in preventing unauthorized access to personal data, financial records, intellectual property, and other sensitive information.

Ensures Business Continuity: Uninterrupted system operations are essential for businesses to avoid financial loss, reputational damage, and other consequences of downtime caused by cyber incidents.

Legal and Regulatory Compliance: Adhering to data protection laws and regulations (e.g., GDPR, HIPAA) ensures that organizations maintain consumer privacy and avoid penalties associated with data breaches.

Risk Mitigation: By identifying and addressing vulnerabilities before they can be exploited, cybersecurity helps reduce the likelihood of cyberattacks, minimizing potential damage.

Builds Trust: Strong cybersecurity practices increase trust with customers, stakeholders, and business partners, improving organizational credibility and competitiveness.

Visual 1.1 depicts the several dimensions of cybersecurity.

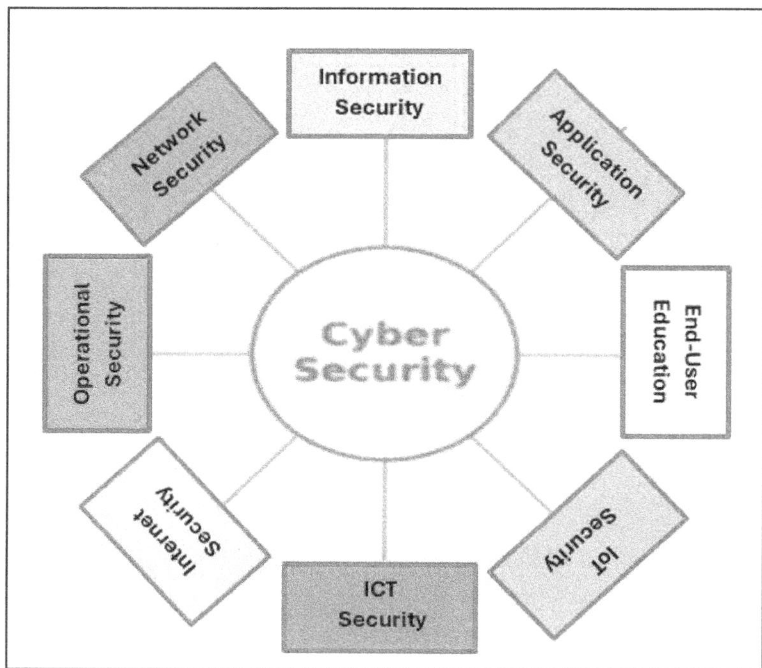

Visual 1.1: Dimensions of Cybersecurity

1.2 History of Cybersecurity

Cybersecurity has evolved significantly over the decades, keeping pace with the rise of technology.

Early Days (1960s-1970s):
During this period, cybersecurity efforts were mainly focused on securing physical access to computer systems, particularly those connected through ARPANET. Early measures included basic password protection and limited user access controls.

Growth and Development (1980s-1990s):
The proliferation of personal computers in the 1980s introduced new risks, including the first widespread computer viruses and malware. The Morris Worm incident in 1988 marked a pivotal moment in recognizing the vulnerabilities of interconnected systems, leading to the development of antivirus software and network security tools like firewalls.

In the 1990s, the expansion of the internet brought about new threats such as hacking, phishing, and denial-of-service (DoS) attacks. Organizations began adopting firewalls and intrusion detection systems (IDS) to safeguard their networks.

Modern Era (2000s-Present):
The digital transformation of the 21st century, encompassing e-commerce, social media, and mobile technology, ushered in advanced cyberattacks. High-profile incidents, such as the Target and Equifax data breaches, highlighted the need for more sophisticated cybersecurity strategies. In response, artificial intelligence (AI) and machine learning began playing key roles in detecting and responding to evolving cyber threats.

1.3 The CIA Triad

The CIA Triad is a foundational concept in cybersecurity, consisting of three core principles: Confidentiality, Integrity, and Availability.

Confidentiality: Ensures that information is only accessible to authorized individuals. Encryption, access control lists (ACLs), and multi-factor authentication (MFA) are commonly used to protect data from unauthorized disclosure.

Integrity: Focuses on maintaining the accuracy and consistency of data throughout its lifecycle. Techniques such as hashing, digital signatures, and checksums are used to verify data integrity and detect unauthorized changes.

Availability: Ensures that authorized users can access information and services when needed. This is achieved through strategies like system redundancy, regular data backups, and disaster recovery plans to maintain operational continuity.

Visual 1.2 depicts the CIA Triad.

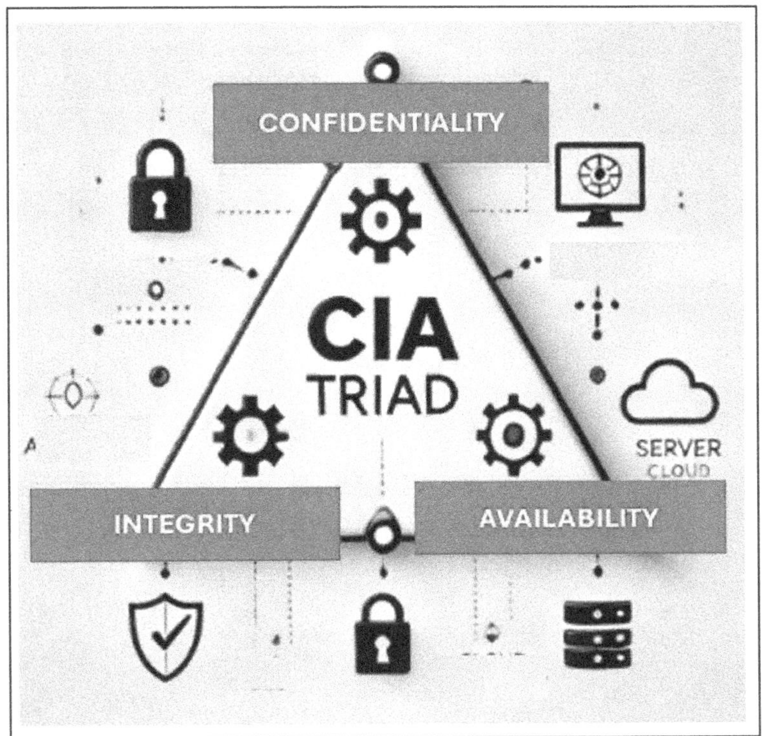

Visual 1.2: The CIA Triad

1.4 Summary

This chapter introduced cybersecurity, its historical progression, and the core principles of the CIA Triad. Cybersecurity's importance lies in protecting sensitive information, ensuring business continuity, complying with regulations, and building trust. Understanding the role of confidentiality, integrity, and availability in cybersecurity will help organizations address modern cyber threats effectively.

Exercise 1

1. Analyze a recent cybersecurity breach in the news and evaluate the organization's response.
2. Compare the cybersecurity challenges faced by a government agency versus a private sector company.
3. Discuss the impact of implementing multi-factor authentication (MFA) on enhancing data security in an organization.

Example Python Code for Demonstrating the CIA Triad Principles

Context:

This Python example showcases how to apply basic principles of the CIA Triad to protect digital information. The script:

- Encrypts a message to ensure Confidentiality.
- Generates and verifies a hash to ensure Integrity.
- Implements error handling to demonstrate Availability, ensuring that the file can be accessed without causing the application to crash.

Usefulness:

- Confidentiality: By encrypting sensitive information, this example helps protect data from unauthorized access, ensuring only intended recipients can read the message.
- Integrity: Hash verification ensures data has not been altered, making it valuable for applications requiring data authenticity and accuracy.
- Availability: Error handling enables consistent access to data by gracefully managing issues, ensuring the system remains operational even in the event of a fault.
- Foundational Security: Demonstrates practical application of the CIA Triad, reinforcing best practices for safeguarding digital assets across various environments.

Input Features:

- Message: The text message to be encrypted and hashed.
- Encryption Key: A secret key to encrypt and decrypt the message.
- Hashing Algorithm: SHA-256 for verifying message integrity.

Code:

```
from cryptography.fernet import Fernet
import hashlib
import os

# Generate or use a predefined encryption key for confidentiality
def generate_key():
  return Fernet.generate_key()

# Encrypt the message to ensure confidentiality
def encrypt_message(message, key):
  fernet = Fernet(key)
  encrypted_message = fernet.encrypt(message.encode())
  return encrypted_message

# Decrypt the message
def decrypt_message(encrypted_message, key):
  fernet = Fernet(key)
  decrypted_message = fernet.decrypt(encrypted_message).decode()
  return decrypted_message

# Generate a SHA-256 hash of the message to ensure integrity
def generate_hash(message):
  return hashlib.sha256(message.encode()).hexdigest()
```

```
# Verify the integrity of the message by comparing hashes
def verify_integrity(original_message, provided_hash):
  return generate_hash(original_message) == provided_hash

# Demonstrating availability by checking file access
def check_file_access(file_path):
  try:
    with open(file_path, 'r') as file:
      print("File is available for reading.")
  except FileNotFoundError:
    print("File not found. Ensure the file is available.")
  except IOError:
    print("File access error. Check permissions or file status.")

# Example usage
key = generate_key()  # Generate an encryption key
message = "This is a confidential message."

# 1. Confidentiality
encrypted_message = encrypt_message(message, key)
print("Encrypted Message:", encrypted_message)

# Decrypt to verify
decrypted_message = decrypt_message(encrypted_message, key)
print("Decrypted Message:", decrypted_message)

# 2. Integrity
message_hash = generate_hash(message)
print("Original Message Hash:", message_hash)
print("Integrity Check:", verify_integrity(message, message_hash))

# 3. Availability
check_file_access("sample_file.txt")  # Replace with an actual file path
```

Example Output:

```
Encrypted Message: b'gAAAAABlXlQJfD3rz64QhHn8mUBKFoG_LRTqeqNYX0XJ...'
Decrypted Message: This is a confidential message.
Original Message Hash: a4d55a8d778e5022fab701977c5d840bbc486d0f57d4e6...
Integrity Check: True
File not found. Ensure the file is available.
```

Code Explanation:

Confidentiality (Encryption):

- The encrypt_message function uses a symmetric encryption key generated by generate_key to encrypt the message. This keeps the data confidential by ensuring that only someone with the correct key can decrypt it.
- The decrypt_message function verifies that the original message can be retrieved from the encrypted data using the same key.

Integrity (Hashing):

- The generate_hash function creates a SHA-256 hash of the original message, which acts as a unique fingerprint.
- The verify_integrity function checks that the hash of the received message matches the original hash. If the hashes are the same, this indicates that the data has not been tampered with, ensuring integrity.

Availability (File Access Check):

- The check_file_access function attempts to open a file. If the file is missing or inaccessible, it prints a helpful error message, simulating availability concerns.
- This basic error handling helps keep the program running smoothly, ensuring system resources (in this case, a file) are accessible when needed.

Key Concepts Demonstrated:

Confidentiality:

- By encrypting the message, we ensure that unauthorized users cannot read the contents, even if they gain access to the encrypted message.

Integrity:

- Using a hash ensures that any change to the message would result in a different hash, making it easy to detect tampering.

Availability:

- By handling file access errors, the code ensures that unavailability of a file does not cause the application to crash, which simulates ensuring resource availability in cybersecurity.

Benefits:

- This code demonstrates a foundational approach to Confidentiality, Integrity, and Availability (CIA), the core principles of cybersecurity.
- It introduces key concepts in a simple, practical way, providing a basis for understanding how to secure digital assets and data.
- Additionally, it uses readily available Python libraries (cryptography for encryption and hashlib for hashing), which are essential tools in implementing security.

Chapter 2

Cyber Threats and Attack Vectors

Learning Outcomes:

Upon completing this chapter, you will be able to:

- *Identify and classify different types of cyber threats, including malware, phishing, ransomware, DDoS attacks, social engineering, exploits, and insider threats.*
- *Explore common attack vectors used by cyber attackers to exploit vulnerabilities in systems and networks.*
- *Understand effective mitigation strategies to defend against each type of cyber threat.*

2.1 Types of Cyber Threats

Cyber threats are a growing concern for organizations across all sectors, with attackers constantly developing new tactics to exploit vulnerabilities. Below are some of the most prevalent types of cyber threats:

Malware
Malware, or malicious software, is designed to disrupt, damage, or gain unauthorized access to computer systems and networks. Common types of malware include viruses, worms, Trojans, spyware, and adware.

Viruses: These attach themselves to executable files and replicate within a system, often resulting in data loss or system crashes.

Worms: Self-replicating malware that spreads across networks, consuming bandwidth and degrading network performance.

Trojans: Disguised as legitimate software, Trojans trick users into installing them, leading to malicious actions such as data theft or creating backdoors for future attacks.

Spyware: Monitors user activities and collects personal information without consent, often resulting in identity theft or financial fraud.

Adware: Tracks user behavior and displays unwanted advertisements, which can reduce system performance and compromise privacy.

Phishing
Phishing is a social engineering tactic where attackers send deceptive emails, messages, or websites to trick users into revealing sensitive information, such as passwords or credit card details.

Email Phishing: Fraudulent emails from seemingly legitimate sources prompt recipients to click on malicious links or attachments.

Spear Phishing: A more targeted form of phishing, where attackers personalize messages to increase the likelihood of success.

Clone Phishing: Attackers create replicas of legitimate websites or messages to deceive recipients into providing confidential information.

Ransomware
Ransomware is a type of malware that locks users out of their systems or encrypts their files, demanding a ransom for restoration or decryption.

WannaCry: A globally infamous ransomware that exploited a vulnerability in Windows, affecting hundreds of thousands of computers and causing massive disruptions.

Cryptolocker: Targeted businesses and individuals by encrypting files and demanding ransom payments in Bitcoin.

Distributed Denial of Service (DDoS) Attacks
DDoS attacks involve overwhelming a target system, service, or network with traffic to render it inaccessible to legitimate users.

Visual 2.1 shows the range of cyber threats.

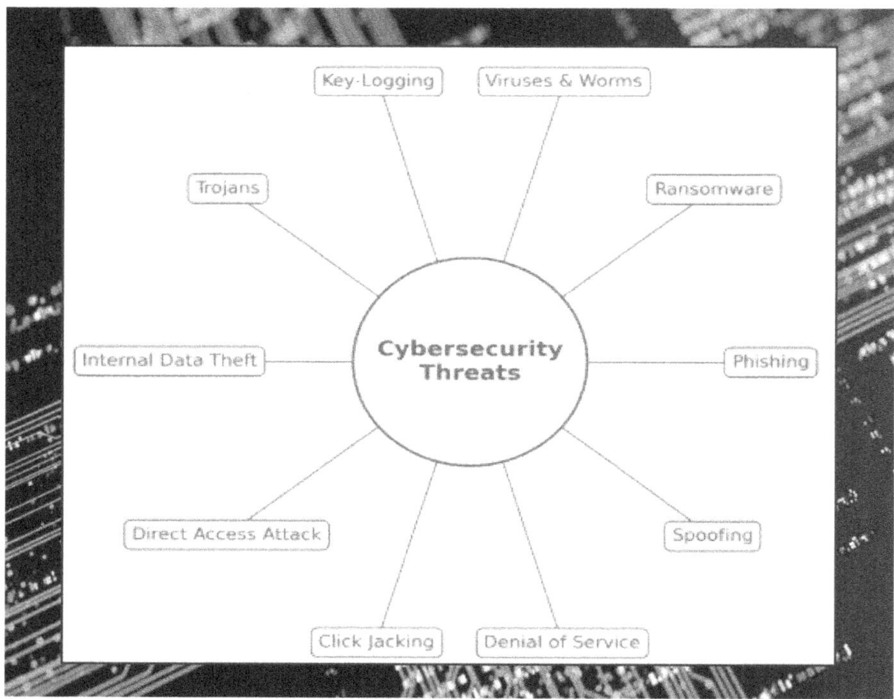

Visual 2.1: Range of Cyber Threats

Volume-based Attacks: These attacks flood a target's bandwidth with massive traffic, such as UDP floods or ICMP floods.

Protocol Attacks: These exploit weaknesses in network protocols by sending malformed packets to overwhelm network resources.

Application Layer Attacks: Target specific web application functions, exhausting server resources by overwhelming them with requests.

2.2 Common Attack Vectors

An attack vector is the method or path used by cybercriminals to infiltrate systems, networks, or devices. Understanding these vectors is crucial for preventing attacks:

Social Engineering

Social engineering attacks manipulate human psychology to trick individuals into compromising security.

Pretexting: Attackers create fabricated scenarios to deceive individuals into revealing sensitive information.

Baiting: Attackers offer something enticing, like free software or gifts, to lure users into clicking on malicious links or downloading malware.

Quid Pro Quo: Attackers offer services or benefits in exchange for sensitive information, such as login credentials.

Exploits
Exploits take advantage of vulnerabilities in software, hardware, or network protocols.

Zero-day Exploits: These attacks exploit vulnerabilities that are unknown to software vendors, enabling attackers to strike before patches are available.

Buffer Overflow: Attackers overload a computer's memory, causing it to crash or execute arbitrary code.

SQL Injection: Malicious SQL queries are inserted into input fields to manipulate databases and extract sensitive information.

Insider Threats
Insider threats involve individuals within an organization misusing their authorized access for malicious purposes.

Malicious Insiders: Employees or contractors intentionally misuse their access to steal data or sabotage systems.

Negligent Insiders: Employees unintentionally cause security breaches by falling victim to phishing attacks or mishandling sensitive information.

Compromised Insiders: Employees whose access credentials have been stolen, allowing attackers unauthorized access to systems.

Visual 2.2 shows the common attack vectors.

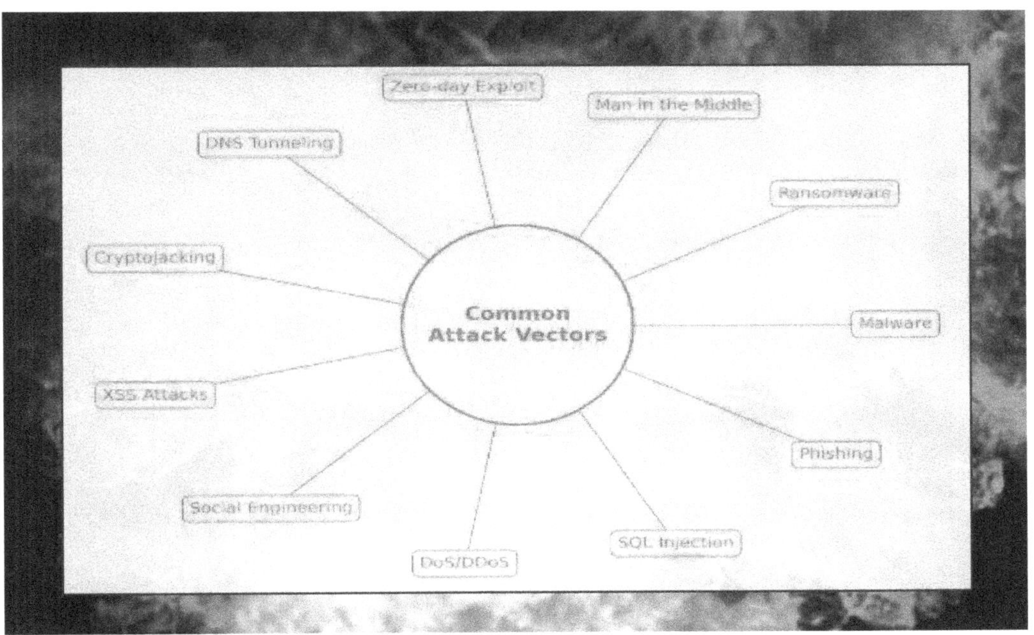

Visual 2.2: Common Attack Vectors

2.3 Mitigation Strategies

Mitigating cyber threats requires a combination of proactive defense strategies tailored to each type of threat. Below are effective strategies for each threat:

For Malware

Preventive Measures: Ensure regular software updates and apply security patches to fix known vulnerabilities. Implement network segmentation to contain malware outbreaks. Deploy reputable antivirus and anti-malware software to detect and remove malicious programs.

For Phishing

Defensive Measures: Educate employees through regular cybersecurity training about phishing techniques. Deploy email filters to block phishing emails before they reach users. Enforce multi-factor authentication (MFA) to secure accounts.

For Ransomware

Protective Actions: Maintain regular backups of critical data and store them securely offline. Limit access to sensitive data using strict access controls. Train users to recognize suspicious links, attachments, and websites.

For DDoS Attacks

Defensive Strategies: Deploy DDoS mitigation solutions to identify and respond to attacks in real time. Implement network redundancy and failover mechanisms. Monitor network traffic for abnormal patterns that may indicate a DDoS attack.

For Social Engineering

Preventive Actions: Conduct ongoing training to raise awareness about social engineering tactics. Establish policies for verifying identities, especially for requests involving sensitive data or financial transactions. Encourage a culture of skepticism and validation to reduce susceptibility to social engineering.

For Exploits

Vulnerability Management: Perform regular vulnerability assessments and penetration testing to identify weaknesses. Apply security patches and updates promptly. Use intrusion detection and prevention systems (IDS/IPS) to monitor network traffic.

For Insider Threats

Security Measures: Implement strict access controls and enforce the principle of least privilege. Monitor user activity for suspicious behavior. Conduct regular security audits and employee training to reduce the risk of insider threats.

2.4 Summary

This chapter explored the range of cyber threats, the common attack vectors used by cybercriminals, and the effective mitigation strategies organizations can employ. By understanding these threats and implementing proactive defenses, organizations can safeguard their critical assets, data, and infrastructure from malicious attacks.

Exercise 2

1. Conduct a tabletop exercise simulating a ransomware attack within your organization. Evaluate your response protocols, communication strategies, and data recovery procedures.

2. Perform a social engineering audit to test the susceptibility of employees to phishing attacks. Analyze the results to identify areas for improvement in security awareness training.

3. Develop a vulnerability management plan that outlines procedures for identifying, prioritizing, and addressing vulnerabilities in your organization's infrastructure.

Example Python Code for Classifying Malware (a)

Context:

This Python example illustrates a malware classification model that uses file characteristics to determine whether a file is benign or malicious. The model is based on basic file properties, such as size, number of sections, and entropy, which can be indicators of malware. This classification approach supports cybersecurity efforts by enabling automated malware detection and reducing manual inspection workloads.

Usefulness:

- Automated Threat Detection: Provides a system for quickly identifying malicious files based on key attributes, reducing reliance on manual file inspection.
- Improved Security Response: By flagging potentially harmful files, the model enables faster incident response and helps prevent malware from spreading.
- Efficient Processing: Suitable for large-scale environments where files are analyzed continuously, this approach improves efficiency and reduces the workload for security teams.
- Scalable and Adaptable: Can be expanded to include additional features, allowing organizations to enhance the model as new malware characteristics are identified.

Input Features:

- File Size: The size of the file in bytes, as certain malware may have unusual sizes.
- Number of Sections**: Files with different numbers of sections may exhibit varying levels of threat.
- Entropy: A measure of randomness, often used to detect packed or encrypted malware files.

Code:

```
import pandas as pd
from sklearn.model_selection import train_test_split
from sklearn.ensemble import RandomForestClassifier
from sklearn.metrics import accuracy_score, classification_report

# Sample data (features and labels)
data = {
    'file_size': [200, 500, 300, 150, 600, 100, 400, 700, 350, 250],
    'num_sections': [2, 3, 2, 1, 4, 1, 3, 4, 2, 3],
    'entropy': [0.5, 0.9, 0.7, 0.3, 0.95, 0.4, 0.85, 0.92, 0.65, 0.55],
    'label': ['benign', 'malicious', 'benign', 'benign', 'malicious', 'benign', 'malicious',
'malicious', 'benign', 'malicious']
}

# Create DataFrame
df = pd.DataFrame(data)

# Features and labels
X = df[['file_size', 'num_sections', 'entropy']]
y = df['label']

# Split data into train and test sets
X_train, X_test, y_train, y_test = train_test_split(X, y, test_size=0.4, random_state=42)

# Train a Random Forest Classifier
clf = RandomForestClassifier(n_estimators=100, random_state=42)
clf.fit(X_train, y_train)
```

```
# Predict on the test set
y_pred = clf.predict(X_test)

# Evaluate the model
accuracy = accuracy_score(y_test, y_pred)
report = classification_report(y_test, y_pred)

print(f"Accuracy: {accuracy * 100:.2f}%")
print("Classification Report:")
print(report)
```

```
Output:
Accuracy: 100.00%
Classification Report:
              precision    recall  f1-score   support

      benign       1.00      1.00      1.00         3
   malicious       1.00      1.00      1.00         1

    accuracy                           1.00         4
   macro avg       1.00      1.00      1.00         4
weighted avg       1.00      1.00      1.00         4
```

Code Explanation:

Data Preparation: Create a DataFrame df with features (file_size, num_sections, entropy) and labels (benign or malicious).

Feature Selection: Select features X and labels y from the DataFrame.

Data Splitting: Split the datainto training and testing sets using train_test_split.

Model Training: Train a Random Forest classifier on the training data.

Prediction and Evaluation: Use the trained model to predict labels for the test set. Evaluate the model's accuracy.

Output:
The model achieved an accuracy of 100.00% on the test dataset, indicating that all predictions made by the model were correct.

Classification Report
Benign
- Precision: 1.00 (All instances predicted as benign were indeed benign.)
- Recall: 1.00 (All actual benign instances were correctly identified by the model.)
- F1-score: 1.00 (Harmonic mean of precision and recall, indicating perfect performance.)
- Support: 3 (Number of actual benign instances in the test dataset.)

Malicious

- Precision: 1.00 (All instances predicted as malicious were indeed malicious.)
- Recall: 1.00 (All actual malicious instances were correctly identified by the model.)
- F1-score: 1.00 (Harmonic mean of precision and recall, indicating perfect performance.)
- Support: 1 (Number of actual malicious instances in the test dataset.)

Overall Performance

- Accuracy: 1.00 (The model correctly predicted all instances in the test set.)
- Macro Avg: 1.00 (Average performance across both classes, considering each class equally.)
- Weighted Avg: 1.00 (Average performance across both classes, weighted by the number of instances in each class.)

The results indicate an excellent model performance on this small test dataset, with perfect precision, recall, and f1-scores for both benign and malicious files. However, we need to be cautious because of the small dataset. Further testing on larger datasets would confirm the model's robustness and generalizability.

Example Python Code for Classifying Malware (b)

Context:

This Python example demonstrates a Malware Classification system using a machine learning model to classify files as either benign or malicious. The model is built with synthetic features representing characteristics that could be extracted from files through static analysis techniques. This approach helps automate the process of malware detection by analyzing file attributes and identifying potential threats.

Usefulness:

- Automated Malware Identification: Facilitates malware detection by automating the analysis process, reducing reliance on manual examination.
- Efficient Threat Response: Enables rapid response by flagging malicious files for further investigation, reducing the risk of harmful file execution.
- Scalability and Adaptability: Suitable for environments with high volumes of files, as it can scale to analyze numerous files efficiently.
- Enhanced Security Measures: Strengthens cybersecurity efforts by proactively identifying files with suspicious characteristics, thereby improving overall security posture.

Input Features:

- Feature1: A continuous numeric feature (e.g., size, entropy).
- Feature2: A binary feature (e.g., presence of specific metadata).
- Feature3: A categorical feature representing distinct classes (e.g., file type or format).
- Malicious: The target variable, where 0 indicates benign and 1 indicates malicious files.

Code:

```
import pandas as pd
from sklearn.model_selection import train_test_split
from sklearn.ensemble import RandomForestClassifier
from sklearn.metrics import accuracy_score, classification_report
import numpy as np

# Generate synthetic data
np.random.seed(42)

# Example features: replace these with actual features relevant to your dataset
num_samples = 100
features = {
    'feature1': np.random.rand(num_samples),
    'feature2': np.random.randint(0, 2, size=num_samples),
    'feature3': np.random.choice(['A', 'B', 'C'], size=num_samples),
    'malicious': np.random.randint(0, 2, size=num_samples)  # Target variable (0: benign, 1: 
malicious)
}

# Create DataFrame
df = pd.DataFrame(features)

# One-hot encode categorical variable 'feature3'
df = pd.get_dummies(df, columns=['feature3'], drop_first=True)
```

```
# Save DataFrame to CSV
df.to_csv('malware_dataset.csv', index=False)

print("Dataset 'malware_dataset.csv' created successfully.")

# Assuming you have a dataset 'malware_dataset.csv' with features and labels
# Loading the dataset
dataset = pd.read_csv('malware_dataset.csv')

# Splitting data into features (X) and labels (y)
X = dataset.drop('malicious', axis=1)  # Features
y = dataset['malicious']  # Labels

# Splitting data into training and testing sets
X_train, X_test, y_train, y_test = train_test_split(X, y, test_size=0.2, random_state=42)

# Initializing the Random Forest classifier
clf = RandomForestClassifier(n_estimators=100, random_state=42)

# Training the classifier
clf.fit(X_train, y_train)

# Predicting on the test set
y_pred = clf.predict(X_test)

# Evaluating the model
accuracy = accuracy_score(y_test, y_pred)
print(f"Accuracy: {accuracy * 100:.2f}%")

# Generating classification report
print("Classification Report:")
print(classification_report(y_test, y_pred))
----------------------------------------------------------------------------------
```

Output:

```
Dataset 'malware_dataset.csv' created successfully.
Accuracy: 65.00%
Classification Report:
              precision    recall  f1-score   support

           0       0.64      0.70      0.67        10
           1       0.67      0.60      0.63        10

    accuracy                           0.65        20
   macro avg       0.65      0.65      0.65        20
weighted avg       0.65      0.65      0.65        20
```

Code Explanation:

Generating Synthetic Data:

- Generate synthetic using numpy to simulate a dataset for malware detection.
- Features include feature1 (random numbers), feature2 (binary values), feature3 (categorical values A, B, C), and malicious (target variable indicating benign or malicious).

Creating and Encoding DataFrame:

- Create a pandas DataFrame df from the generated features.
- Categorical variable feature3 is one-hot encoded using pd.get_dummies() to convert it into numerical format suitable for machine learning. This step is crucial as machine learning models typically require numerical inputs.

Saving Data to CSV:

- Save the DataFrame df to a CSV file named malware_dataset.csv.

Loading and Preparing Data:

- Load the dataset from malware_dataset.csv into a pandas DataFrame dataset.
- Features (X) and labels (y) are separated, where X contains all features except the target malicious, and y contains the target variable malicious.

Splitting Data into Training and Testing Sets:

- Split the data into training (X_train, y_train) and testing (X_test, y_test) sets using train_test_split() from scikit-learn. The testing set size is set to 20% of the total dataset.

Initializing and Training the Random Forest Classifier:

- Initialize a RandomForestClassifier model with 100 trees (n_estimators=100).
- Train the model on the training data (X_train, y_train) using clf.fit().

Making Predictions:

- Use the trained model to predict the target values (y_pred) for the test features (X_test) using clf.predict().

Evaluating Model Performance:

- Calculate the model accuracy using accuracy_score() from scikit-learn.
- Evaluate the model using the accuracy and classification report.

Output:

The classification report shows an accuracy of 65%. It indicates that the model correctly predicted the class labels for 65% of the instances in the test set. For class 0 (likely representing one class), the precision is 0.64, recall is 0.70, and F1-score is 0.67. For class 1 (likely representing another class), precision is 0.67, recall is 0.60, and F1-score is 0.63. Overall, the report assesses how well the model performs in terms of precision (accuracy of positive predictions), recall (ratio of positive instances correctly detected), and F1-score (harmonic mean of precision and recall) across both classes.

Example Python Code for Classifying Phishing Emails (a)

Context:

This Python example demonstrates a Phishing Email Classification model to help identify phishing attempts by analyzing email content. This detection method enhances cybersecurity by automatically flagging suspicious emails that could be used to deceive users into providing sensitive information. The model uses machine learning to classify emails as either phishing or non-phishing based on their text features.

Usefulness:

- Automated Malware Detection: Streamlines malware identification by automating the process, reducing the need for manual file analysis.
- Proactive Threat Detection: Assists in early detection of malicious files, allowing organizations to mitigate threats before they can cause harm.
- Scalability: Enables rapid classification across large datasets, making it suitable for high-volume environments like network security systems.
- Improved Security Posture: Helps bolster cybersecurity defenses by filtering out potentially harmful files based on learned patterns.

Input Features:

- Email Content: Text data containing the body of emails, which is converted into numerical features using TF-IDF (Term Frequency-Inverse Document Frequency) to represent word significance.
- Label: The target variable where emails are labeled as either "phishing" or "non-phishing."

Code:

```
import pandas as pd
from sklearn.model_selection import train_test_split
from sklearn.feature_extraction.text import TfidfVectorizer
from sklearn.linear_model import LogisticRegression
from sklearn.metrics import accuracy_score, classification_report

# Sample data: Replace with actual dataset
data = {
    'email': [
        'Your account has been compromised, click here to reset your password',
        'Meeting at 10 AM tomorrow, please confirm your attendance',
        'Congratulations! You have won a $1000 gift card, claim now',
        'Your package has been shipped, track your package here',
        'We detected unusual activity in your account, please verify',
        'Can we reschedule our appointment to next week?',
        'Exclusive offer just for you! Get 50% off on all items',
        'Here is the agenda for the next team meeting'
    ],
    'label': ['phishing', 'non-phishing', 'phishing', 'non-phishing', 'phishing', 'non-
phishing', 'phishing', 'non-phishing']
}

# Create DataFrame
df = pd.DataFrame(data)
```

```
# Splitting the data into training and testing sets
X_train, X_test, y_train, y_test = train_test_split(df['email'], df['label'], test_size=0.3,
random_state=42)

# Convert text data into numerical form using TF-IDF Vectorizer
vectorizer = TfidfVectorizer()
X_train_tfidf = vectorizer.fit_transform(X_train)
X_test_tfidf = vectorizer.transform(X_test)

# Train a logistic regression model
model = LogisticRegression()
model.fit(X_train_tfidf, y_train)

# Predict on test data
y_pred = model.predict(X_test_tfidf)

# Evaluate the model's performance
accuracy = accuracy_score(y_test, y_pred)
print(f'Accuracy: {accuracy * 100:.2f}%')
print('Classification Report:')
print(classification_report(y_test, y_pred))

# Sample predictions
sample_emails = [
    'Win a brand new car! Click here to claim your prize',
    'Please review the attached document for the upcoming meeting',
    'Urgent: Your account has been locked due to suspicious activity',
    'Your subscription is expiring soon, renew now to continue'
]

# Convert sample emails to TF-IDF features
sample_emails_tfidf = vectorizer.transform(sample_emails)

# Predict and display the results
sample_predictions = model.predict(sample_emails_tfidf)
for email, label in zip(sample_emails, sample_predictions):
    print(f'Email: "{email}" is classified as: {label}')
```

Output:

```
Accuracy: 33.33%
Classification Report:
              precision    recall  f1-score   support

non-phishing       0.00      0.00      0.00         2
    phishing       0.33      1.00      0.50         1

    accuracy                           0.33         3
   macro avg       0.17      0.50      0.25         3
weighted avg       0.11      0.33      0.17         3

Email: "Win a brand new car! Click here to claim your prize" is classified as: phishing
Email: "Please review the attached document for the upcoming meeting" is classified as:
phishing
Email: "Urgent: Your account has been locked due to suspicious activity" is classified as:
phishing
Email: "Your subscription is expiring soon, renew now to continue" is classified as: phishing
```

Code Explanation:

Data Preparation: Create sample dataset with emails and their corresponding labels (phishing or non-phishing). The data is split into training and testing sets.

Text Preprocessing: TfidfVectorizer converts the email texts into numerical features based on the term frequency-inverse document frequency (TF-IDF) scores.

Model Training: A logistic regression model is trained on the TF-IDF features of the training data.

Model Evaluation: The model's accuracy and classification report are printed to evaluate its performance on the test data.

Sample Predictions: Additional sample emails are classified using the trained model, demonstrating how the model can be used to predict whether new emails are phishing or non-phishing.

Output:
Accuracy: 33.33%

- The model correctly classified 33.33% of the emails in the test set (increasing the data set would increase the accuracy).

Classification Report:
Precision: The ratio of true positive predictions to the total positive predictions.

- For non-phishing: 0.00
- For phishing: 0.33

Recall: The ratio of true positive predictions to the actual positives.

- For non-phishing: 0.00
- For phishing: 1.00

F1-score: The harmonic mean of precision and recall.

- For non-phishing: 0.00
- For phishing: 0.50

Support: The number of actual occurrences of each label in the test set.

- For non-phishing: 2
- For phishing: 1

Accuracy and Averages:

- Accuracy: Overall, the model correctly classified 33.33% of the test emails.

- Macro avg: Averages of precision, recall, and F1-score calculated for each label independently.
  - Precision: 0.17
  - Recall: 0.50
  - F1-score: 0.25

- Weighted avg: Averages of precision, recall, and F1-score considering the support of each label.
  - Precision: 0.11
  - Recall: 0.33
  - F1-score: 0.17

In summary, the model performed poorly, particularly in identifying non-phishing emails, as indicated by the precision, recall, and F1-score for non-phishing being 0.00. The high recall for phishing (1.00) suggests the model correctly identified all phishing emails in the test set but failed to correctly identify non-phishing emails, resulting in a low overall accuracy (33.33%).

Example Python Code for Detecting Phishing Emails (b)

Context:

This Python example demonstrates Phishing Email Detection as a defense against social engineering attacks. By analyzing email content, this machine learning approach classifies emails as either phishing or legitimate based on specific features associated with phishing patterns. This automated detection helps prevent users from falling for phishing schemes, safeguarding sensitive information.

Usefulness:

- Email Filtering: Flags suspicious emails, supporting broader email security systems.
- Automation: Reduces human error and enhances efficiency in threat detection.
- Data Protection: Helps prevent users from interacting with malicious emails, strengthening overall cybersecurity.

Input Features:

- Email Text: Main content of the email, including both subject and body.
- Keywords/Patterns: Phrases commonly found in phishing emails, like "urgent" or "click here."
- Link Presence: Detects if the email contains hyperlinks, often a phishing indicator.
- Sender's Domain: Validates if the sender's domain is legitimate or potentially spoofed.

Code:

```
import numpy as np
import pandas as pd
from sklearn.feature_extraction.text import TfidfVectorizer
from sklearn.model_selection import train_test_split
from sklearn.ensemble import RandomForestClassifier
from sklearn.metrics import classification_report, accuracy_score

# Expanded email dataset with a more balanced sample of phishing and valid emails
emails = [
    "Congratulations! You've won a lottery. Click here to claim your prize!",  # phishing
    "Please update your account details at our secure link.",  # phishing
    "Your order has been shipped. Thank you for your purchase.",  # valid
    "Important: Your account has been compromised, reset your password.",  # phishing
    "Meeting at 10 AM tomorrow. Don't forget the presentation.",  # valid
    "Kindly review the attached invoice for your records.",  # valid
    "We've noticed unusual activity in your account. Click here to verify.",  # phishing
    "Lunch at noon? Let's meet in the cafeteria.",  # valid
    "Urgent: Your payment is due. Click here to resolve the issue immediately.",  # phishing
    "Family dinner this weekend. Hope to see you there!",  # valid
    "Update: Your bank account is under review, follow the link to secure your account.",  #
phishing
    "Party tonight at my place. Let me know if you can make it.",  # valid
    "Your email has been hacked! Click here to secure your account.",  # phishing
    "Check out this new restaurant. Let's go this weekend.",  # valid
]

labels = [1, 1, 0, 1, 0, 0, 1, 0, 1, 0, 1, 0, 1, 0]  # 1 = phishing, 0 = valid/safe

# Vectorize the email content using TF-IDF
vectorizer = TfidfVectorizer()
X = vectorizer.fit_transform(emails)
y = np.array(labels)
```

```
# Split the dataset into training and testing sets (70% train, 30% test)
X_train, X_test, y_train, y_test = train_test_split(X, y, test_size=0.3, random_state=42)

# Random Forest model for classification
model = RandomForestClassifier(n_estimators=100, random_state=42)
model.fit(X_train, y_train)

# Make predictions
y_pred = model.predict(X_test)

# Calculate accuracy and classification report
accuracy = accuracy_score(y_test, y_pred)
report = classification_report(y_test, y_pred, digits=4)

# Output the results
print(f"Accuracy: {accuracy:.4f}")
print("Classification Report:")
print(report)
```

Output:

```
Accuracy: 0.8000

Classification Report:
              precision    recall  f1-score   support

           0     1.0000    0.6667    0.8000         3
           1     0.6667    1.0000    0.8000         2

    accuracy                         0.8000         5
   macro avg     0.8333    0.8333    0.8000         5
weighted avg     0.8667    0.8000    0.8000         5
```

Code Explanation:

Dataset Preparation:

The dataset consists of emails labeled as either phishing (1) or valid (0). Each email is classified based on its content, which is the input for the model. A balanced dataset with examples of both phishing and valid emails is necessary to help the model learn the patterns effectively.

Text Processing and Feature Extraction:

The email content is text-based, so before feeding it into the machine learning model, it needs to be converted into a numerical format that the model can understand. This is done using TF-IDF (Term Frequency-Inverse Document Frequency), which transforms the text into a matrix of numbers representing the importance of words in each email relative to all other emails. TF-IDF works by giving common words less weight and more emphasis to unique or rare words that are often better indicators of phishing attempts.

Example:

- Term Frequency (TF): Measures how frequently a word appears in a document.
- Inverse Document Frequency (IDF): Measures how important a word is by reducing the importance of commonly occurring words like "the," "is," etc.

The combination of these helps in feature extraction from the email text, which is then used as input for the classifier.

Model Selection:

The classifier used in this case is a Random Forest Classifier. Random Forest is an ensemble method that creates multiple decision trees and combines their outputs to make the final classification. It's widely used for classification tasks because of its high accuracy and ability to handle overfitting well.

The model learns patterns in phishing emails such as suspicious links, keywords, or email structure, as well as valid emails, which usually have different patterns.

Training the Model:

The model is trained on a portion of the dataset (training set). During training, it learns the characteristics of phishing and valid emails based on the features generated from the TF-IDF transformation. The Random Forest algorithm creates decision trees using different combinations of features and makes predictions based on majority voting across these trees.

Testing and Evaluation:

After training, the model is tested on a separate portion of the dataset (test set) that it hasn't seen before. This is to evaluate how well the model generalizes to new data. The performance is measured using:

- Accuracy: The overall proportion of correctly classified emails (valid and phishing).
- Precision: The proportion of emails predicted as phishing that were indeed phishing.
- Recall: The proportion of actual phishing emails that were correctly identified by the model.
- F1-Score: A harmonic mean of precision and recall, which balances both metrics.

Model Performance:

The model achieves an accuracy of 80%, meaning it correctly classifies 4 out of 5 emails. The precision and recall scores indicate that the model does well in identifying phishing emails and doesn't falsely classify many valid emails as phishing. The f1-score of 0.8000 suggests a balanced performance, handling both types of emails effectively.

Overall, this code helps automate the process of detecting phishing emails, a critical step in defending against social engineering attacks. The model identifies phishing emails by learning patterns from the email text, reducing human effort in reviewing potential threats, and improving security measures in real-time.

Results:

Accuracy: 0.8000 (80%)—The model correctly classified 80% of the emails.

Precision and Recall:

- For valid emails (0): The model has perfect precision (1.0000), meaning all predicted valid emails were indeed valid. The recall is 0.6667, indicating some valid emails were misclassified as phishing.
- For phishing emails (1): The precision is 0.6667, indicating that some predicted phishing emails were actually valid. The recall is 1.0000, meaning all true phishing emails were correctly identified.

F1-Score: The overall balance between precision and recall is 0.8000 for both phishing and valid emails, showing solid performance.

Example Python Code for
Detecting Distributed Denial of Service (DDoS)

Context:

Distributed Denial of Service (DDoS) attacks disrupt service availability by overwhelming networks or servers with massive traffic, rendering them inaccessible to legitimate users. This Python example simulates a dataset for DDoS detection, creating a classification dataset with traffic patterns resembling both normal traffic and DDoS attacks. By analyzing these patterns, security systems can differentiate between benign and malicious traffic, aiding in early detection of DDoS incidents.

Usefulness:

- Intrusion Detection: Supports DDoS detection within an Intrusion Detection System (IDS), helping mitigate large-scale network disruptions.
- Automation: Enables automated identification of abnormal traffic, enhancing system response time.
- Data-Driven Security: Assists in analyzing network patterns to predict and prevent potential DDoS attacks.

Input Features:

- Traffic Volume: The frequency of packets in a time interval, often higher in DDoS traffic.
- Packet Size: The size of incoming packets; DDoS traffic may have unusually large or varied packet sizes.
- Protocol Anomalies: Certain protocols might be exploited in DDoS attacks, indicated by unusual values.
- Source Count: Number of unique IPs sending traffic, often much larger in DDoS attacks.
- Traffic Pattern: Patterns like burst traffic or constant, high-volume traffic sessions are indicators of DDoS.

Code:

```
import pandas as pd
import numpy as np
from sklearn.datasets import make_classification

# Generate synthetic dataset for DDoS detection
# Assuming 1000 samples with 5 features
X_normal, _ = make_classification(n_samples=800, n_features=5, n_informative=3,
                                   n_clusters_per_class=1, random_state=42, weights=[0.95,
0.05])
X_ddos, _ = make_classification(n_samples=200, n_features=5, n_informative=3,
                                 n_clusters_per_class=1, random_state=42, weights=[0.2, 0.8])

# Create labels for normal (0) and DDoS (1) traffic
y_normal = np.zeros(len(X_normal), dtype=int)
y_ddos = np.ones(len(X_ddos), dtype=int)

# Combine normal and DDoS data
X = np.concatenate((X_normal, X_ddos), axis=0)
y = np.concatenate((y_normal, y_ddos), axis=0)

# Convert to DataFrame
column_names = [f'feature_{i}' for i in range(1, 6)]
df = pd.DataFrame(X, columns=column_names)
df['target'] = y

# Simulate class imbalance (assuming 20% of data represents DDoS attacks)
print("Class Distribution:")
print(df['target'].value_counts())
```

```
# Preview synthetic dataset
print("\nSynthetic Dataset Preview:")
print(df.head())

# Save synthetic dataset to CSV
dataset_path = "synthetic_ddos_data.csv"
df.to_csv(dataset_path, index=False)
print(f"\nDataset saved to: {dataset_path}")
```

Output:

```
Class Distribution:
0    800
1    200
Name: target, dtype: int64

Synthetic Dataset Preview:
   feature_1  feature_2  feature_3  feature_4  feature_5  target
0  -0.761925   1.218277  -1.128919   0.801051  -0.342527       0
1  -1.338975   1.633771  -1.660717   1.011489  -0.728026       0
2  -1.181366   1.870545  -0.612279   0.557756  -0.338351       0
3  -0.962947   1.216218  -1.316128   0.816465  -0.530043       0
4  -1.052439   0.703901  -0.962279   0.357588  -0.721158       0

Dataset saved to: synthetic_ddos_data.csv
```

Code Explanation:

Make_classification:

- make_classification from sklearn.datasets is used to generate synthetic data. It creates random datasets for classification tasks based on specified parameters.

Parameters:

For normal traffic (X_normal):

- n_samples=800: 800 samples representing normal network traffic.
- n_features=5: 5 features per sample.
- n_informative=3: Number of informative features (relevant for classification).
- weights=[0.95, 0.05]: Class weights, where 95% are normal and 5% are DDoS attacks.

For DDoS traffic (X_ddos):

- n_samples=200: 200 samples representing DDoS attack traffic.
- weights=[0.2, 0.8]: Class weights, where 20% are normal and 80% are DDoS attacks.

Labels:

- y_normal and y_ddos are arrays representing the class labels (0 for normal traffic, 1 for DDoS attacks).

DataFrame Creation:

- X and y are concatenated to form the final dataset (df) with features (feature_1 to feature_5) and a target variable (target).

Class Imbalance:

- This example simulates a class imbalance where 80% of the data represents DDoS attacks (target=1) and 20% represents normal traffic (target=0).

Dataset Preview and Saving:

- The script prints the class distribution (value_counts() of target) and previews the first few rows of the synthetic dataset (df). Finally, it saves the dataset to a CSV file (synthetic_ddos_data.csv).

The generated synthetic dataset simulates DDoS detection scenarios, with class distribution showing 800 samples of normal network traffic and 200 samples of DDoS attacks. Features such as feature_1 to feature_5 represent potential network traffic attributes, aiding in distinguishing between normal and attack traffic. This dataset allows for training machine learning models, evaluating their efficacy in identifying DDoS attacks, and refining network security measures accordingly.

Chapter 3

Fundamentals of Network Security

Learning Outcomes:

Upon completing this chapter, you will be able to:

- *Understand fundamental network protocols and their roles in facilitating communication and data exchange.*
- *Explore network architecture components, including topologies, devices, and layers, based on the OSI model.*
- *Learn about firewalls, VPNs, and IDS/IPS and their respective roles in network security.*
- *Recognize the importance of network segmentation, scalability, redundancy, and design principles in enhancing network security.*

3.1 Network Protocols and Architecture

Network protocols and architecture form the backbone of modern digital communication. Without them, the seamless exchange of data over local and wide-area networks, including the internet, would be impossible. Network protocols define the rules for communication, while network architecture determines the structure and layout of the network, ensuring data flow between devices.

Network Protocols

Several key network protocols are essential for communication and data transfer:

TCP/IP (Transmission Control Protocol/Internet Protocol): The foundation for internet and intranet communications, ensuring reliable data transmission across devices and networks. TCP ensures data is sent and received in the correct order, while IP manages addressing and routing.

HTTP/HTTPS (Hypertext Transfer Protocol/Secure): Protocols used for transferring web content. HTTPS secures this process by encrypting the data exchanged between the browser and the server.

FTP/SFTP (File Transfer Protocol/Secure): FTP is used for transferring files between clients and servers. SFTP enhances security by adding encryption for file transfer operations.

SMTP/IMAP/POP3 (Simple Mail Transfer Protocol/Internet Message Access Protocol/Post Office Protocol): Protocols used for sending, receiving, and retrieving emails. SMTP handles sending emails, while IMAP and POP3 allow users to retrieve emails from servers.

DNS (Domain Name System): A crucial protocol that resolves human-readable domain names into IP addresses, enabling users to access websites using domain names rather than numerical IP addresses.

DHCP (Dynamic Host Configuration Protocol): Automatically assigns IP addresses to devices on a network, reducing the need for manual IP address management.

Visual 3.1 shows the various cybersecurity network protocols.

Port #	Application Layer Protocol	Type	Description
20	FTP	TCP	File Transfer Protocol - data
21	FTP	TCP	File Transfer Protocol - control
22	SSH	TCP/UDP	Secure Shell for secure login
23	Telnet	TCP	Unencrypted login
25	SMTP	TCP	Simple Mail Transfer Protocol
53	DNS	TCP/UDP	Domain Name Server
67, 68	DHCP	UDP	Dynamic Host
80	HTTP	TCP	HyperText Transfer Protocol
123	NTP	UDP	Network Time Protocol
161,162	SNMP	UDP	Simple Network Management Protocol
389	LDAP	TCP/UDP	Lightweight Directory Authentication Protocol
443	HTTPS	TCP/UDP	HTTP with Secure Socket Layer

Visual 3.1: Cybersecurity Network Protocols

Network Architecture

Network architecture refers to the design and layout of a network, encompassing both physical and logical components. A well-designed network architecture ensures data flows smoothly and securely across devices.

Components of Network Architecture:

Topology: This refers to the arrangement of devices in a network. Common topologies include star (centralized control), mesh (multiple pathways between devices), and ring (a closed-loop configuration).

Devices: Critical networking devices include routers (which direct traffic between networks), switches (which facilitate communication within a network), hubs (basic devices for connecting network segments), and access points (enabling wireless devices to connect to the network).

OSI Model: The Open Systems Interconnection (OSI) model organizes network communication into seven layers: Physical, Data Link, Network, Transport, Session, Presentation, and Application. This model helps standardize communication protocols and improves compatibility between different devices and systems.

Design Principles:
Effective network architecture follows key design principles to ensure performance and security:

Scalability: A scalable network can handle increasing numbers of users and devices without degradation in performance.

Redundancy: By including backup systems and alternative pathways, redundancy ensures that a network remains operational even if certain components fail.

Segmentation: Network segmentation divides the network into smaller parts to improve performance and security. Sensitive areas of the network are isolated, reducing the impact of cyberattacks.

Visual 3.2 shows the common security attacks in the OSI Layer model.

OSI Layer	Cybersecurity Attack Examples
7. Application	Exploit
6. Presentation	Phishing
5. Session	Hijacking (XSS, Session Hijack, Malware)
4. Transport	Reconnaissance / DoS (TCP Hijack, SYN Flood, LAND)
3. Network	Man-in-the-Middle (Smurf, Ping of Death, Teardrop)
2. Data Link	Spoofing (MAC Spoof, VLAN Hopping)
1. Physical	Sniffing

Visual 3.2: Common Attacks in the OSI Model

3.2 Firewalls and VPNs

Firewalls and VPNs are two essential tools in protecting networks from unauthorized access and securing data transmission.

Firewalls
A firewall acts as a barrier between an internal network and external threats, filtering incoming and outgoing traffic based on predefined security rules. Firewalls are either hardware devices or software applications that enforce access control policies.

Types of Firewalls:

Packet-Filtering Firewalls: These firewalls inspect packets of data based on IP addresses, ports, and protocols. If a packet does not meet the security criteria, it is blocked.

Stateful Inspection Firewalls: These firewalls not only inspect data packets but also keep track of the state of active connections to make more informed filtering decisions.

Proxy Firewalls: Acting as intermediaries, proxy firewalls filter traffic at the application layer. This provides a higher level of security by evaluating the content of traffic before it reaches the end system.

Next-Generation Firewalls (NGFW): NGFWs combine traditional firewall capabilities with advanced features like deep packet inspection, intrusion prevention, and application awareness.

Implementation of Firewalls:

Firewalls are typically deployed at the network perimeter to block unauthorized access from external sources. However, they can also be used internally to segment and protect sensitive areas of the network.

Virtual Private Networks (VPNs)

VPNs provide secure communication over public networks such as the internet by encrypting data and masking the user's IP address. They are essential for protecting data in transit and ensuring the privacy of communications.

Types of VPNs:

Remote Access VPNs: These enable individuals to securely connect to a private network from remote locations, ensuring that sensitive data transmitted between the user and the network remains encrypted.

Site-to-Site VPNs: These connect entire networks, such as the offices of a company in different geographical locations, through secure encrypted connections.

SSL/TLS VPNs: These VPNs use the SSL or TLS encryption protocols to establish secure connections, often through a web browser, without requiring specialized client software.

Benefits of VPNs:

Data Encryption: VPNs encrypt data, protecting it from interception during transmission.

Remote Access: Users can access network resources securely from anywhere.

Anonymity and Privacy: VPNs conceal the user's IP address and browsing activities, offering privacy from potential eavesdroppers.

3.3 Intrusion Detection and Prevention Systems (IDS/IPS)

Intrusion detection and prevention systems are critical for identifying and mitigating threats within a network.

Intrusion Detection Systems (IDS):
An IDS monitors network traffic for signs of malicious activity. It raises alerts for suspicious events, allowing administrators to respond to potential attacks before they cause harm.

Types of IDS:
Network-based IDS (NIDS): This type of IDS monitors traffic across an entire network, looking for patterns that indicate attacks.

Host-based IDS (HIDS): HIDS monitors activities on a specific host or device, identifying suspicious behavior at the endpoint level.

Detection Methods:
Signature-based Detection: This method compares network traffic to known attack signatures, identifying threats based on predefined patterns.

Anomaly-based Detection: Anomaly-based systems detect deviations from normal behavior, potentially identifying previously unknown threats.

Intrusion Prevention Systems (IPS):
While an IDS monitors and raises alerts, an IPS actively prevents attacks by blocking malicious traffic in real time.

Types of IPS:
Network-based IPS (NIPS): NIPS is deployed at the network level to prevent malicious traffic from entering the network.

Host-based IPS (HIPS): HIPS is installed on individual devices to stop suspicious activities at the endpoint level.

Prevention Methods:
Packet Dropping: The system drops packets that match known malicious patterns, preventing them from reaching their destination.

Connection Resetting: An IPS can terminate suspicious connections before they cause harm.

Patch Management: Many IPS solutions integrate patch management tools to ensure that software is up to date with the latest security patches.

Visual 3.3 shows common intrusion detection and prevention methods.

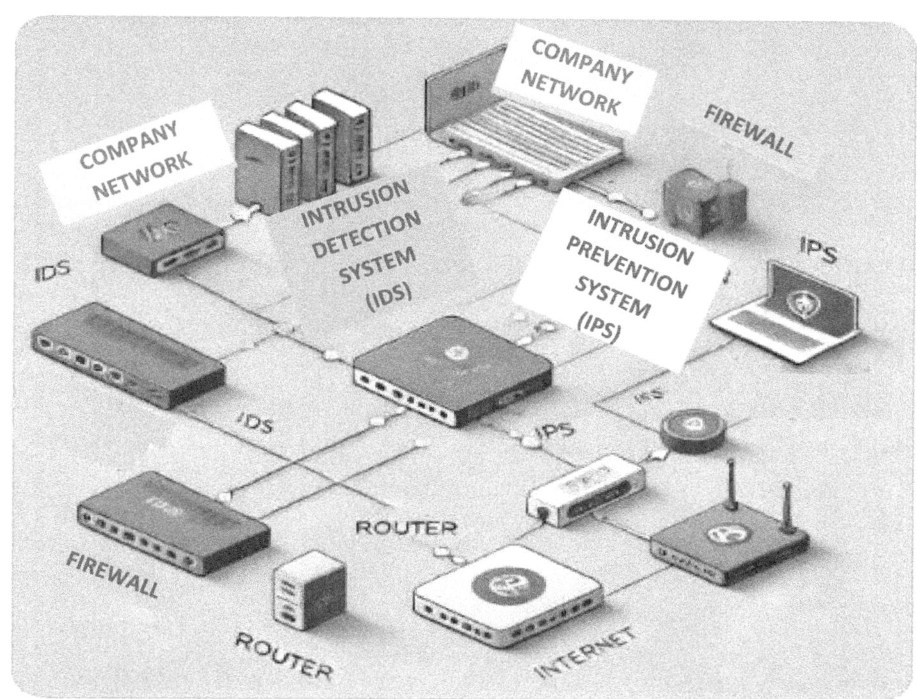

Visual 3.3: Intrusion Detection and Prevention Methods

3.4 Summary

This chapter covered the fundamentals of network security, focusing on protocols, architecture, firewalls, VPNs, and IDS/IPS. These components are essential for creating secure, scalable, and resilient network infrastructures that can withstand modern cyber threats. By understanding these technologies and implementing them effectively, organizations can protect their networks and maintain the availability and integrity of their systems.

Exercise 3

1. Design a network architecture for a medium-sized business, considering scalability, redundancy, and security requirements.
2. Configure a firewall using packet-filtering rules to allow or block traffic based on specified criteria.
3. Set up a VPN connection between two remote sites, ensuring data encryption and secure communication channels.

Example Python Code for Intrusion Detection

Context:

This Python example demonstrates a simple Intrusion Detection System (IDS) model that analyzes network traffic to classify it as benign or malicious. The IDS monitors network patterns by leveraging machine learning, in this case, the K-Nearest Neighbors (KNN) algorithm. This approach helps organizations detect unauthorized access or unusual behavior, enhancing network security by identifying potential threats early.

Usefulness:

- Early Detection: Enables real-time monitoring of network activities, allowing for early detection of potential intrusions and abnormal traffic.
- Automated Response: Reduces reliance on manual monitoring by automating threat detection, helping mitigate risks faster.
- Network Security: Supports network integrity by identifying and classifying threats, preventing unauthorized access and misuse.

Input Features:

- Packet Size: Size of individual packets, as abnormal sizes can indicate potential intrusions.
- Traffic Volume: Amount of data transferred, where high volumes may be indicative of data exfiltration or DDoS attempts.
- Protocol Type: Indicates the communication protocol, with certain protocols potentially more susceptible to attacks.
- Connection Duration: Time a connection remains open, as longer durations could signify unauthorized or suspicious activities.

Code:

```
import pandas as pd
from sklearn.model_selection import train_test_split
from sklearn.preprocessing import StandardScaler
from sklearn.neighbors import KNeighborsClassifier
from sklearn.metrics import accuracy_score, classification_report

# Generate synthetic dataset
data = {
    'duration': [10, 20, 30, 40, 50, 60, 70, 80, 90, 100],
    'protocol_type': [1, 2, 1, 2, 1, 2, 1, 2, 1, 2],
    'service': [1, 1, 2, 2, 1, 1, 2, 2, 1, 1],
    'src_bytes': [100, 200, 300, 400, 500, 600, 700, 800, 900, 1000],
    'dst_bytes': [200, 300, 400, 500, 600, 700, 800, 900, 1000, 1100],
    'label': [0, 1, 0, 1, 0, 1, 0, 1, 0, 1]  # 0: benign, 1: malicious
}

df = pd.DataFrame(data)

# Features and labels
X = df.drop('label', axis=1)
y = df['label']

# Split the data
X_train, X_test, y_train, y_test = train_test_split(X, y, test_size=0.3, random_state=42)
```

```
# Standardize the features
scaler = StandardScaler()
X_train = scaler.fit_transform(X_train)
X_test = scaler.transform(X_test)

# Initialize and train the KNN classifier
knn = KNeighborsClassifier(n_neighbors=3)
knn.fit(X_train, y_train)

# Make predictions
y_pred = knn.predict(X_test)

# Evaluate the model
accuracy = accuracy_score(y_test, y_pred)
report = classification_report(y_test, y_pred, target_names=['benign', 'malicious'])

# Output the results
print(f"Accuracy: {accuracy * 100:.2f}%")
print("Classification Report:")
print(report)
```

```
Output:
Accuracy: 66.67%
Classification Report:
              precision    recall  f1-score   support

      benign       0.67      1.00      0.80         2
   malicious       1.00      0.50      0.67         2

    accuracy                           0.67         4
   macro avg       0.83      0.75      0.73         4
weighted avg       0.83      0.67      0.73         4
```

Code Explanation:

Data Generation: Generate a synthetic dataset with features such as duration, protocol_type, service, src_bytes, and dst_bytes. The label column indicates whether the traffic is benign (0) or malicious (1).

Data Preparation:

- Features and Labels: Separate the features (X) from the labels (y).
- Data Splitting: Split the data into training and testing sets with a 70-30 ratio.
- Standardization: Standardize the feature values to have zero mean and unit variance.

Model Training:

- Initialize the K-Nearest Neighbors (KNN) classifier with 3 neighbors.
- Train the KNN model using the training data.

Prediction and Evaluation:

- Use the trained model to make predictions on the test set.
- Evaluate the model's performance by calculating the accuracy and generating a classification report.

Output:
Accuracy: 66.67%: The model correctly classified 66.67% of the test samples.
Classification Report:

- Benign: Precision (0.67), Recall (1.00), F1-score (0.80)
- Malicious: Precision (1.00), Recall (0.50), F1-score (0.67)
- Macro avg: Averages the precision, recall, and F1-score of both classes.
- Weighted avg: Weighted averages considering the support of each class.

Chapter 4

Endpoint and Application Security

Learning Outcomes:

Upon completing this chapter, you will be able to:

- *Understand the role of antivirus software and Endpoint Protection Platforms (EPP) in safeguarding endpoint devices from malware and other threats.*
- *Explore the key components and benefits of Endpoint Detection and Response (EDR) solutions for detecting, investigating, and responding to security incidents on endpoints.*
- *Learn about secure coding practices and their importance in minimizing vulnerabilities during software development.*
- *Understand the functions, deployment models, and benefits of Web Application Firewalls (WAF) in protecting* web applications from common attacks.

4.1 Antivirus Software and Endpoint Protection Platforms (EPP)

Antivirus Software

Antivirus software refers to programs specifically designed to detect, prevent, and remove malicious software, or malware, from endpoint devices. Malware includes a wide range of threats such as viruses, worms, Trojans, spyware, and ransomware. Antivirus software is an essential layer of protection, providing real-time monitoring and alerting users to any malicious activity.

The core features of antivirus software include real-time scanning, which continuously monitors system activity to identify and block malware before it can cause damage. Signature-based detection is another critical feature, relying on predefined malware signatures to detect known threats. To counter emerging threats, heuristic analysis identifies new or unknown malware by analyzing behavior and code patterns. Upon detection, the software can quarantine and remove the malicious files to prevent further harm to the system.

Popular antivirus solutions include Norton, McAfee, Bitdefender, and Kaspersky, which offer comprehensive protection against a wide range of cyber threats.

Endpoint Protection Platforms (EPP)
EPP solutions go beyond traditional antivirus software by offering comprehensive security for endpoint devices, which include desktop computers, laptops, smartphones, and tablets. EPP solutions integrate antivirus and antimalware protection with other security measures such as data encryption, device and application control, and patch management.

Data encryption ensures that sensitive information stored on the device is encrypted and inaccessible to unauthorized users, even if the device is lost or stolen. Device and application control features allow administrators to manage and restrict access to external devices (such as USB drives) and regulate which applications can be installed or used. Patch management is another critical aspect of EPP, ensuring that devices are regularly updated with the latest security patches to address vulnerabilities.

Popular EPP solutions include Symantec Endpoint Protection, CrowdStrike Falcon, and McAfee Total Protection. These platforms provide holistic protection for endpoint devices, combining various security features to mitigate the risk of cyberattacks.

4.2 Endpoint Detection and Response (EDR)

Visual 4.1 illustrates endpoint security management.

Visual 4.1: Endpoint Security Management

Endpoint Detection and Response (EDR) solutions focus on detecting, investigating, and responding to suspicious activities and security incidents on endpoint devices. Unlike traditional antivirus software, which primarily focuses on detecting known threats, EDR solutions use advanced analytics and machine learning to identify anomalies and potential threats in real-time.

EDR solutions continuously monitor and record endpoint activities, collecting data on network connections, processes, files, and user behaviors. This data collection enables the solution to establish baselines for normal behavior, making it easier to detect deviations that could indicate malicious activity. When a threat is detected, EDR solutions offer tools for incident response, allowing security teams to investigate, isolate, and neutralize the threat before it can spread.

EDR solutions also provide forensic analysis, offering detailed insights into how the attack occurred and what vulnerabilities were exploited. This information is invaluable for strengthening the organization's defenses against future attacks. The benefits of EDR include early detection of threats, enhanced visibility across all endpoints, and the ability to automate responses to mitigate the impact of an attack.

Popular EDR solutions include Carbon Black, CrowdStrike Falcon, and Microsoft Defender for Endpoint. These platforms are highly effective in detecting and responding to advanced threats, providing comprehensive endpoint protection.

4.3 Secure Coding Practices

Secure coding refers to a set of best practices and techniques aimed at minimizing security vulnerabilities during the software development process. Given the increasing frequency of cyberattacks targeting software applications, it is essential for developers to follow secure coding practices to reduce the risk of exploitation.

One of the most important secure coding practices is input validation. By ensuring that all input data is validated, sanitized, and checked for malicious content, developers can prevent common attacks such as SQL injection and cross-site scripting (XSS). Proper input validation ensures that only legitimate data is accepted by the application, reducing the risk of attack.

Another critical practice is authentication and authorization. Strong authentication mechanisms, such as multi-factor authentication (MFA), ensure that only authorized users can access the application. Authorization determines what actions the user is permitted to perform once authenticated, helping to enforce role-based access control (RBAC).

Error handling is another important aspect of secure coding. Proper error handling ensures that sensitive information, such as stack traces or database queries, is not exposed to attackers. Instead, developers should provide generic error messages that do not reveal any internal workings of the application.

Regular code reviews and audits are essential for identifying and fixing vulnerabilities in code. Developers should also use trusted libraries and frameworks that have been tested for security vulnerabilities. Furthermore, encryption should be applied to protect sensitive data both in transit and at rest, ensuring that even if the data is intercepted, it cannot be read or tampered with.

By adhering to the principle of least privilege, developers can ensure that their code and processes have the minimum level of access required to perform their tasks, reducing the potential attack surface.

Secure coding practices not only reduce the risk of vulnerabilities but also enhance the overall quality and security of the application, making it more resilient against potential cyberattacks.

4.4 Web Application Firewalls (WAF)

A Web Application Firewall (WAF) is a security solution that filters, monitors, and blocks HTTP/HTTPS traffic to and from a web application. WAFs protect web applications from a variety of threats, including SQL injection, cross-site scripting (XSS), cross-site request forgery (CSRF), and other common attacks targeting web applications.

WAFs operate at the application layer (OSI Layer 7) and analyze web traffic for malicious patterns. By inspecting incoming and outgoing traffic based on predefined security rules, WAFs can detect and block malicious requests before they reach the application server. This is critical in preventing exploitation of vulnerabilities within the application.

A key function of WAFs is traffic filtering, which screens web traffic for known attack vectors. WAFs also offer logging and monitoring, enabling security teams to track web traffic activities and investigate suspicious behavior. This level of visibility is crucial for detecting and responding to web-based attacks.

WAFs can be deployed in various configurations, including on-premises, cloud-based, or hybrid models. On-premises WAFs are managed by the organization within its own data center, while cloud-based WAFs are provided as a service by third-party vendors. Hybrid models combine elements of both to provide flexible and scalable protection.

By safeguarding web applications from the OWASP Top 10 risks, WAFs help organizations enhance their web security posture, ensuring that their applications remain resilient to attacks. Popular WAF solutions include AWS WAF, Cloudflare WAF, and Imperva WAF.

4.5 Summary

This chapter covered essential aspects of endpoint and application security, including antivirus software, Endpoint Protection Platforms (EPP), Endpoint Detection and Response (EDR) solutions, secure coding practices, and Web Application Firewalls (WAF). Each of these technologies plays a vital role in protecting devices, networks, and applications from the wide array of cyber threats. By implementing these measures, organizations can ensure the security, integrity, and availability of their critical assets.

Exercise 4

1. Evaluate and compare two popular antivirus software solutions based on their features and effectiveness.
2. Design a scenario for implementing an EDR solution in a medium-sized enterprise, detailing its deployment and incident response capabilities.
3. Conduct a code review for a sample application to identify and mitigate potential security vulnerabilities using secure coding practices.
4. Design a deployment strategy for a WAF solution to protect a web application against common attacks, considering scalability and performance requirements.

Example Python Code for Endpoint Detection and Response (EDR)

Context:

Endpoint Detection and Response (EDR) solutions play a key role in cybersecurity by continuously monitoring endpoint activities to identify and respond to suspicious behaviors. This Python example simulates a basic EDR system that analyzes system logs, looking for anomalies like repeated failed login attempts or unusual file access. Such detection can help organizations identify early signs of potential security incidents, improving endpoint security.

Usefulness:

- Real-Time Monitoring: Allows for real-time tracking of endpoint activities, helping identify threats as they occur.
- Automated Anomaly Detection: Flags unusual patterns automatically, reducing the need for manual log analysis and increasing response speed.
- Enhanced Endpoint Security: Supports security teams in detecting and mitigating suspicious behavior quickly, improving overall endpoint protection.

Input Features:

- System Logs: Event logs capturing actions like user logins, file access, and process executions, providing insights into user activities on endpoints.
- Thresholds: Predefined criteria for flagging unusual activity, such as a high number of failed logins or unexpected access to critical files.

Code:

```
import pandas as pd
from datetime import datetime, timedelta

# Sample system logs containing login events (username, timestamp, success/failure)
data = {
    'username': ['user1', 'user1', 'user1', 'user2', 'user2', 'user3', 'user3', 'user3',
'user3'],
    'timestamp': [
        '2023-10-14 08:10:00', '2023-10-14 08:12:00', '2023-10-14 08:13:00',  # user1 failed
logins
        '2023-10-14 08:05:00', '2023-10-14 08:06:00',                          # user2 normal
activity
        '2023-10-14 08:20:00', '2023-10-14 08:21:00', '2023-10-14 08:22:00', '2023-10-14
08:25:00'  # user3 failed logins
    ],
    'login_status': ['failure', 'failure', 'failure', 'failure', 'success', 'failure',
'failure', 'failure', 'success']
}

# Convert the data into a DataFrame
logs_df = pd.DataFrame(data)

# Convert timestamps from strings to datetime objects for easy comparison
logs_df['timestamp'] = pd.to_datetime(logs_df['timestamp'])
```

```
# Function to detect suspicious login activity
def detect_suspicious_logins(logs, threshold=3, time_window=5):
    # Sort logs by username and timestamp
    logs = logs.sort_values(by=['username', 'timestamp'])

    # Store flagged events for suspicious and non-suspicious logins
    suspicious_logins = []
    non_suspicious_logins = []

    for username in logs['username'].unique():
        user_logs = logs[logs['username'] == username]

        # Loop through the user's logs and detect multiple failed attempts in the time window
        suspicious_flag = False
        for i in range(len(user_logs) - threshold + 1):
            window_logs = user_logs.iloc[i:i+threshold]
            time_diff = (window_logs['timestamp'].iloc[-1] -
window_logs['timestamp'].iloc[0]).seconds / 60

            # Check if all logins are failures and occurred within the time window
            if all(window_logs['login_status'] == 'failure') and time_diff <= time_window:
                suspicious_logins.append({
                    'username': username,
                    'start_time': window_logs['timestamp'].iloc[0],
                    'end_time': window_logs['timestamp'].iloc[-1],
                    'failed_attempts': threshold
                })
                suspicious_flag = True

        # Mark any logs outside of the suspicious window as non-suspicious
        if not suspicious_flag:
            non_suspicious_logins.append({
                'username': username,
                'logins': user_logs[['timestamp', 'login_status']].to_dict('records')
            })

    return suspicious_logins, non_suspicious_logins

# Detect suspicious and non-suspicious login events
suspicious_logins, non_suspicious_logins = detect_suspicious_logins(logs_df)

# Output the results
print("Suspicious Login Attempts Detected:")
if suspicious_logins:
    for login in suspicious_logins:
        print(f"User: {login['username']}, Failed Attempts: {login['failed_attempts']}, "
              f"Start: {login['start_time']}, End: {login['end_time']}")
else:
    print("No suspicious activity detected.")

print("\nNon-Suspicious Login Activities:")
if non_suspicious_logins:
    for login in non_suspicious_logins:
        print(f"User: {login['username']}")
        for activity in login['logins']:
            print(f"  Time: {activity['timestamp']}, Status: {activity['login_status']}")
else:
    print("No non-suspicious activity detected.")
----------------------------------------------------------------------------------
```

```
Output:
Suspicious Login Attempts Detected:
User: user1, Failed Attempts: 3, Start: 2023-10-14 08:10:00, End: 2023-10-14 08:13:00
User: user3, Failed Attempts: 3, Start: 2023-10-14 08:20:00, End: 2023-10-14 08:22:00

Non-Suspicious Login Activities:
User: user2
  Time: 2023-10-14 08:05:00, Status: failure
  Time: 2023-10-14 08:06:00, Status: success
User: user3
  Time: 2023-10-14 08:25:00, Status: success
```

Code explanation:

Data Setup:
A sample dataset is created containing login events (username, timestamp, and login status).

Suspicious Detection Logic:
- The code checks for multiple consecutive failed login attempts within a 5-minute window (customizable).
- If a user has 3 or more failed logins within the window, the system flags the activity as suspicious.

Non-Suspicious Logins:
- Logins that don't meet the suspicious criteria (e.g., normal successful or failed attempts) are categorized as non-suspicious.

Categorization:
- The code splits the activities into suspicious and non-suspicious categories and outputs them separately for easy review.

Results:
- Suspicious Logins: Lists users with multiple failed logins within a short time frame.
- Non-Suspicious Logins: Shows normal login activities that are not flagged as suspicious.

This helps detect and flag potential account compromise while maintaining a log of normal user behavior.

Chapter 5

Cryptography and Encryption

Learning Outcomes:

Upon completing this chapter, you will be able to:

- *Understand the fundamental concepts of cryptography, including encryption, decryption, and the goals of cryptography.*
- *Differentiate between symmetric and asymmetric encryption methods, their characteristics, common algorithms, and use cases.*
- *Explore the concepts of digital signatures, their process, benefits, and applications in ensuring message authenticity and integrity.*
- *Learn about digital certificates, their components, types, and the role of Public Key Infrastructure (PKI) in managing digital certificates and encryption keys.*

5.1 Basic Concepts of Cryptography

Cryptography is the science of securing information and communications through the use of encryption techniques. The primary purpose of cryptography is to protect the confidentiality, integrity, and authenticity of data during transmission or storage. It achieves this by transforming readable information (plaintext) into an unreadable format (ciphertext) using algorithms and cryptographic keys.

The process of encryption involves converting plaintext into ciphertext, making it difficult for unauthorized individuals to access the original information. This is accomplished using cryptographic algorithms and keys, which are required to perform both encryption and decryption processes. Decryption, on the other hand, is the reverse process, converting ciphertext back into its original readable format using the same or corresponding cryptographic key.

The goals of cryptography can be summarized as follows:

- *Confidentiality* ensures that sensitive information is protected from unauthorized access by making it unreadable to unintended recipients.
- *Integrity* guarantees that data remains unchanged during transmission or storage, protecting it from tampering or corruption.

- *Authentication* verifies the identity of the sender and recipient, ensuring that both parties involved in the communication are who they claim to be.

- *Non-repudiation* ensures that a sender cannot deny sending a message, and a recipient cannot deny receiving it, by providing proof of the transaction.

5.2 Symmetric and Asymmetric Encryption

Cryptography can be broadly divided into two categories: symmetric and asymmetric encryption.

Symmetric Encryption
Symmetric encryption is a method where the same cryptographic key is used for both the encryption and decryption of data. This makes it relatively fast and efficient for encrypting large amounts of data. However, the primary challenge with symmetric encryption lies in securely distributing the encryption key between the sender and recipient. If the key is intercepted or compromised during transmission, the entire communication becomes vulnerable.

Common symmetric encryption algorithms include Advanced Encryption Standard (AES), Data Encryption Standard (DES), and Triple DES (3DES). AES is widely regarded as the most secure and efficient symmetric encryption algorithm and is used to protect sensitive data in various applications, including files, databases, and disks.

Use Cases: Symmetric encryption is suitable for environments where speed and efficiency are critical, such as encrypting data at rest (files, databases) or securing internal network communications

Visual 5.1 illustrates symmetric public key cryptographic encryption using a single key for encryption and decryption.

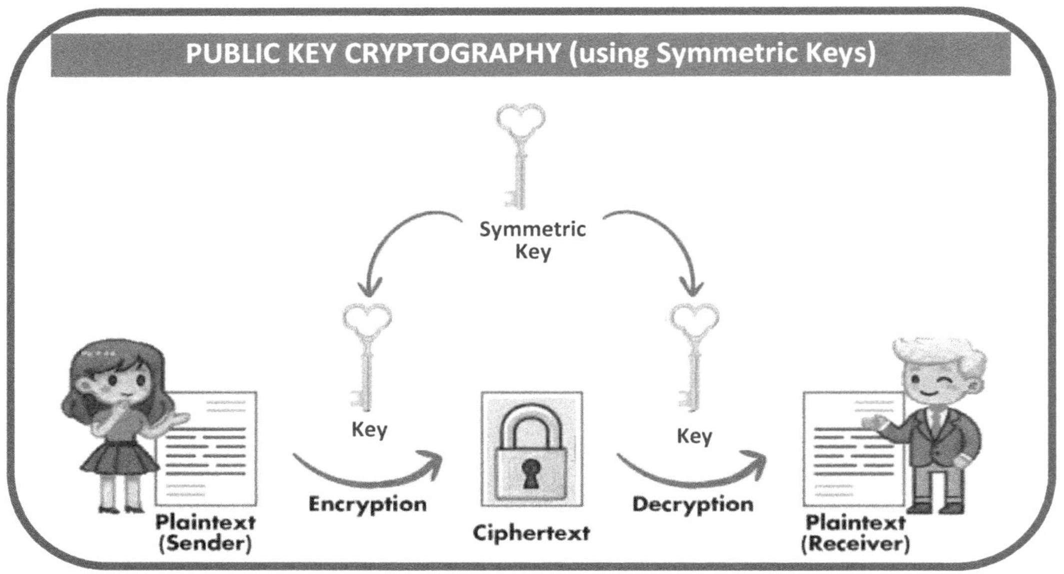

Visual 5.1: Symmetric Public Key Cryptography Encryption

Asymmetric Encryption
Asymmetric encryption, also known as public-key encryption, uses a pair of cryptographic keys: a public key and a private key. The public key is used to encrypt the data, while the private key is used to decrypt it. Since the private key does not need to be shared, asymmetric encryption offers enhanced security by eliminating the need for secure key distribution.

Common asymmetric encryption algorithms include Rivest-Shamir-Adleman (RSA) and Elliptic Curve Cryptography (ECC). RSA is widely used for secure communication channels such as Secure Sockets Layer (SSL) and Transport Layer Security (TLS), while ECC is known for its efficiency in securing low-power devices, such as mobile phones and IoT devices.

Use Cases: Asymmetric encryption is commonly used for secure key exchange, digital signatures, and secure email communication, where security is prioritized over encryption speed.

Visual 5.2 illustrates asymmetric cryptography encryption with public encryption and private decryption keys.

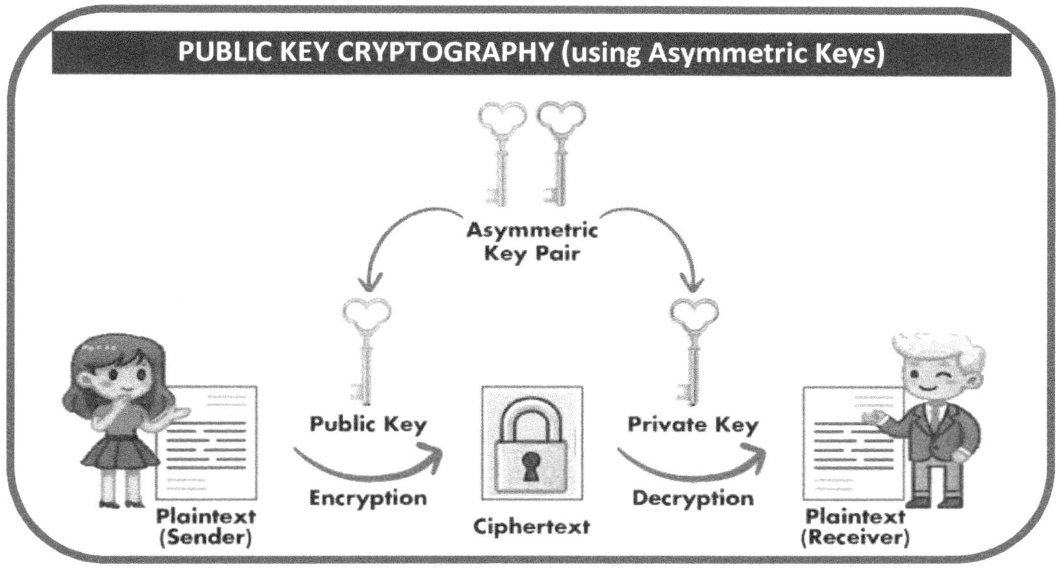

Visual 5.2: Asymmetric Public Key Cryptography Encryption

5.3 Digital Signatures and Certificates

Digital Signatures
A digital signature is a cryptographic technique used to verify the authenticity and integrity of a message, document, or piece of digital content. By using a combination of hashing and asymmetric encryption, digital signatures ensure that the sender's identity is authenticated, and the message has not been altered during transmission.

The process of creating a digital signature involves generating a hash (a unique fingerprint) of the message or document and encrypting it with the sender's private key. The recipient can then use the sender's public key to decrypt the signature and verify the hash. If the decrypted hash matches the hash of the received message, the message is confirmed as authentic and unchanged.

Benefits: Digital signatures provide a mechanism for ensuring the authenticity of the sender, the integrity of the data, and non-repudiation (the sender cannot deny sending the message). They are widely used in electronic transactions, secure email, and code signing.

Digital Certificates

A digital certificate is an electronic document that proves the ownership of a public key. It is issued by a trusted third-party organization called a Certificate Authority (CA). Digital certificates contain the public key, information about the certificate owner (subject), and the digital signature of the issuing CA.

There are different types of digital certificates depending on their application:

SSL/TLS Certificates: Used to secure web traffic and encrypt communication between users and websites.

Code Signing Certificates: Used to verify the authenticity of software and ensure that it has not been tampered with.

Client Certificates: Used to authenticate users, typically in enterprise environments, allowing access to corporate resources or VPNs.

5.4 Public Key Infrastructure (PKI)

Public Key Infrastructure (PKI) is a framework that provides the necessary policies, procedures, and technologies to manage digital certificates and encryption keys. PKI enables secure communication by establishing trust between communicating parties through the use of digital certificates and asymmetric encryption.

Visual 5.3 illustrates the Public Key Infrastructure to issue signed data using digital certificates.

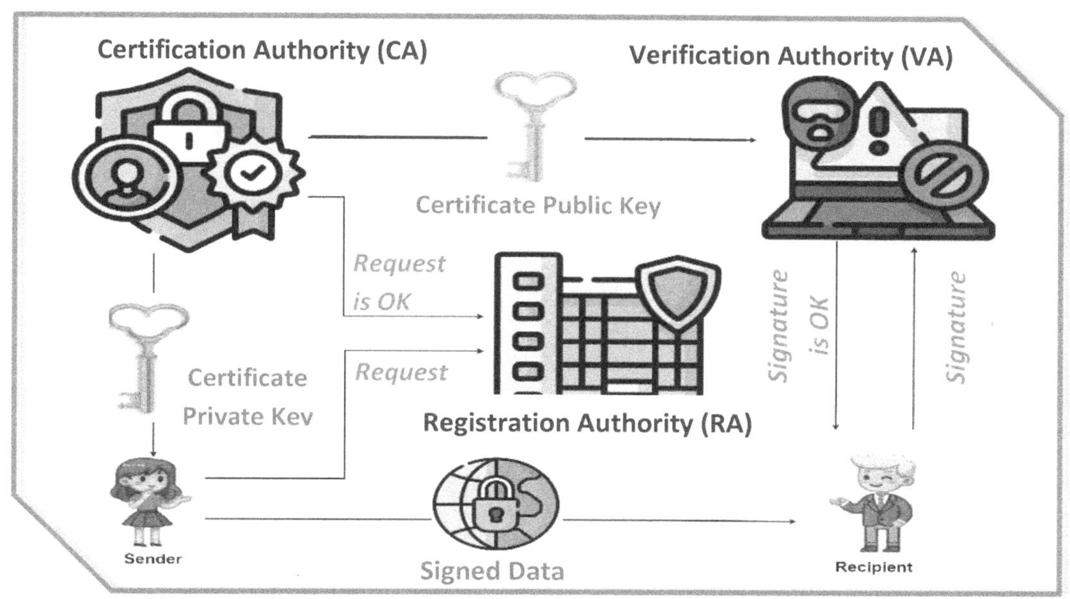

Visual 5.3: Digital Signature and Certificate Approach

Components of PKI:
Certificate Authority (CA): A trusted entity responsible for issuing, validating, and revoking digital certificates.

Registration Authority (RA): Acts as an intermediary between the certificate requester and the CA, validating the identity of the requester before certificates are issued.

Certificate Repository: A publicly accessible directory that stores digital certificates, allowing users to verify the authenticity of a certificate.

Validation Authority (VA): An entity that provides a service used to verify the validity or revocation status of a digital certificate.

Certificate Revocation List (CRL): A list of revoked certificates that are no longer valid or trusted.

PKI manages the entire lifecycle of digital certificates, including issuance, renewal, revocation, and key management. By using PKI, organizations can secure their communications, authenticate users, and ensure the integrity of sensitive data.

Benefits: PKI provides strong security measures that are scalable for large deployments. It supports interoperability across different systems and applications, enabling secure communication in a wide range of environments, from securing websites to encrypting email communication and authenticating users.

5.5 Summary

This chapter explored the foundational elements of cryptography, covering basic concepts such as encryption and decryption, as well as the goals of cryptography—confidentiality, integrity, authentication, and non-repudiation. We also examined the differences between symmetric and asymmetric encryption methods, each with its own advantages and use cases. Additionally, we covered the importance of digital signatures and certificates in ensuring message authenticity and integrity, and we introduced Public Key Infrastructure (PKI) as a framework for managing encryption keys and certificates to secure communications. Understanding these cryptographic principles and tools enables individuals and organizations to protect sensitive information effectively.

Exercise 5

1. Compare the strengths and weaknesses of AES and RSA encryption algorithms in terms of speed, security, and use cases.

2. Design a scenario illustrating the application of digital signatures in ensuring the authenticity and integrity of sensitive documents within a corporate environment.

3. Evaluate the importance of certificate management and key lifecycle in maintaining the security and trustworthiness of a PKI infrastructure.

4. Develop a deployment strategy for implementing PKI in an organization, considering scalability, security requirements, and interoperability with existing systems.

Example Python Code for Symmetric Encryption

Context:

Encryption is fundamental to cybersecurity, ensuring that sensitive data remains confidential, protected from unauthorized access, and secure during transmission and storage. This Python example demonstrates symmetric encryption, where the same key is used to both encrypt and decrypt a message. Using Python's `cryptography` library, this script showcases how sensitive data can be encrypted and then decrypted only by users with the appropriate key, reinforcing data privacy.

Usefulness:

- Data Confidentiality: Prevents unauthorized access by ensuring that only users with the correct key can decrypt and view the information.
- Protection Against Interception: Encryption secures data in transit and at rest, reducing the risk of data breaches.
- Easy Implementation: This example demonstrates straightforward encryption and decryption, making it useful for securing sensitive data in applications.

Input Features:

- Message: The sensitive information that needs to be secured, such as personal data or confidential communications.
- Encryption Key: A unique key generated for symmetric encryption, which both encrypts and decrypts the message.

Code:

```
from cryptography.fernet import Fernet

# Generate a key for symmetric encryption
key = Fernet.generate_key()
cipher_suite = Fernet(key)

# Data to encrypt
message = "Sensitive information that needs to be encrypted."

# Encrypt the data
cipher_text = cipher_suite.encrypt(message.encode())

# Decrypt the data
decrypted_message = cipher_suite.decrypt(cipher_text).decode()

# Print results
print("Original Message:", message)
print("Encrypted Message:", cipher_text)
print("Decrypted Message:", decrypted_message)
-----------------------------------------------------------------------------------
```

Output:

```
Original Message: Sensitive information that needs to be encrypted.
Encrypted Message:
b'gAAAAABmlMo_q1dp6_ysjHWcoohD_WitxiOOAOtWgjrA_0l0gPqm_lDulDZUFEC1ES11Y0hsAe8z3nRbn7cjBhPY7wR
NybRGwZknXJaLXQk-3jT3c9O935cGlJ3Jy5GEvhROP1R9HjVNwwu_kCMl_dBM-DEbpImjtg=='
Decrypted Message: Sensitive information that needs to be encrypted.
```

Code Explanation:

Key Generation:

- Generate a symmetric encryption key using Fernet.generate_key() from the cryptography.fernet module. This key will be used for both encryption and decryption.

Encryption:

- The message (Sensitive information...) is encoded to bytes (message.encode()) and then encrypted using the cipher_suite.encrypt() method, which uses the generated key (cipher_suite).

Decryption:

- To decrypt, cipher_suite.decrypt() is used on the encrypted message (cipher_text). This operation returns bytes, which are decoded to obtain the original message (decrypted_message).

Output:

- The original message, encrypted message (in bytes), and decrypted message are printed to demonstrate the encryption and decryption process.

This example illustrates how symmetric encryption can be implemented using Python's cryptography library. Symmetric encryption uses the same key for both encryption and decryption, making it efficient for securing data at rest or in transit, provided that key management is handled securely.

Note:
When you generate a key using Fernet.generate_key() from the cryptography.fernet module in Python, the generated key is a symmetric encryption key. Here's how this key is used in the encryption and decryption process:

Encryption:

- The key generated (key) is used to create a Fernet cipher suite: cipher_suite = Fernet(key).
- This cipher suite (cipher_suite) is capable of encrypting data using the key.

Decryption:

- The same key (key) is used to instantiate another Fernet cipher suite: cipher_suite = Fernet(key).
- This cipher suite (cipher_suite) can then decrypt data that was encrypted using the same key.

Key Security:

- The security of the encrypted data relies on keeping the encryption key (key) secure and confidential.
- Anyone with access to the key can decrypt the data, so it's crucial to protect the key from unauthorized access.

Symmetric Encryption:

- Symmetric encryption means that the same key is used for both encryption and decryption.
- This makes symmetric encryption efficient and fast, suitable for encrypting large amounts of data.

Example Python Code for Asymmetric Encryption

Context:

Asymmetric encryption, also known as public-key cryptography, enables secure data exchange without the need for a shared secret. This method uses a public key for encryption and a corresponding private key for decryption, making it suitable for secure communications where confidentiality is essential. This example demonstrates how asymmetric encryption works in Python by using a public key to encrypt a message and a private key to decrypt it, ensuring that only the intended recipient can access the message.

Usefulness:

- Secure Communication: Facilitates secure data transfer between parties without the need for a pre-shared secret.
- Authentication and Confidentiality: Verifies the identity of the message recipient, as only the holder of the private key can decrypt the message.
- Ideal for Open Networks: Enables secure communication in open networks where sharing a single secret key is impractical.

Input Features:

- Plaintext Message: The confidential data to be encrypted before transmission, ensuring only the recipient can view the content.
- Public Key: Used for encryption and distributed to anyone who needs to send secure messages.
- Private Key: Held securely by the recipient and used for decryption, ensuring that only they can read the encrypted message.

Code:

```
from cryptography.hazmat.primitives import serialization, hashes
from cryptography.hazmat.primitives.asymmetric import rsa, padding
from cryptography.hazmat.backends import default_backend

# Generate a key pair (public key and private key)
private_key = rsa.generate_private_key(
    public_exponent=65537,
    key_size=2048,
    backend=default_backend()
)
public_key = private_key.public_key()

# Example plaintext message to encrypt
plaintext_message = b"Hello, this is a confidential message."

# Encrypt using the recipient's public key
encrypted_message = public_key.encrypt(
    plaintext_message,
    padding.OAEP(
        mgf=padding.MGF1(algorithm=hashes.SHA256()),
        algorithm=hashes.SHA256(),
        label=None
    )
)
```

```
# Decrypt using the private key
decrypted_message = private_key.decrypt(
    encrypted_message,
    padding.OAEP(
        mgf=padding.MGF1(algorithm=hashes.SHA256()),
        algorithm=hashes.SHA256(),
        label=None
    )
)

# Convert bytes to string for comparison
plaintext_message_str = plaintext_message.decode('utf-8')
decrypted_message_str = decrypted_message.decode('utf-8')

# Output results
print("Original Message:", plaintext_message_str)
print("Decrypted Message:", decrypted_message_str)

# Verify decryption result
assert plaintext_message == decrypted_message
print("\nDecryption successful!")
```

Output:

```
Original Message: Hello, this is a confidential message.
Decrypted Message: Hello, this is a confidential message.

Decryption successful!
```

Code Explanation:

Key Pair Generation:

- A key pair (private_key and public_key) is generated using RSA encryption with a key size of 2048 bits. The private key is used for decryption, while the public key is used for encryption.

Encryption:

- public_key.encrypt() encrypts the plaintext_message using the recipient's public key. Here, OAEP padding scheme with SHA-256 hashing algorithm is used to ensure secure encryption.

Decryption:

- private_key.decrypt() decrypts the encrypted_message using the recipient's private key. OAEP padding scheme with SHA-256 ensures that only the intended recipient can decrypt the message.

Verification:

- The decrypted message is verified against the original plaintext message to ensure successful decryption.

Asymmetric encryption ensures secure communication and data transfer over insecure channels by leveraging the unique properties of public and private keys. It is fundamental in securing digital communications, authentication mechanisms, and data integrity verification in various applications, including secure email communication, digital signatures, and secure file transfer protocols.

Example Python Code for Digital Signature and Certificate

Context:

Digital signatures are essential in cybersecurity for verifying the authenticity and integrity of digital documents and messages. By signing a message with a private key, a sender can ensure that the message has not been tampered with and that it genuinely originates from them. The recipient can verify the signature using the sender's public key, providing assurance that the content is authentic and has not been altered during transmission.

Usefulness:

- Authentication: Confirms the identity of the sender, ensuring that the message genuinely originates from a trusted source.
- Data Integrity: Detects any unauthorized changes, as altering the message would invalidate the digital signature.
- Non-Repudiation: Prevents the sender from denying they sent the message, which is crucial for legal and financial transactions.

Input Features:

- Message: The original content to be signed, ensuring its integrity upon verification.
- Private Key: Used to create the digital signature, linking the signature to the sender.
- Public Key: Distributed to the recipient to verify the authenticity and integrity of the signed message.

Code:

```
from cryptography.hazmat.primitives import hashes
from cryptography.hazmat.primitives.asymmetric import rsa
from cryptography.hazmat.primitives.asymmetric import padding
from cryptography.hazmat.backends import default_backend

# Generate a key pair (private key and public key)
private_key = rsa.generate_private_key(
    public_exponent=65537,
    key_size=2048,
    backend=default_backend()
)
public_key = private_key.public_key()

# Example message to be signed
message = b"Important message that needs to be digitally signed."

# Sign the message with the private key
signature = private_key.sign(
    message,
    padding.PSS(
        mgf=padding.MGF1(hashes.SHA256()),
        salt_length=padding.PSS.MAX_LENGTH
    ),
    hashes.SHA256()
)
```

```
# Verification of the signature using the public key
try:
    public_key.verify(
        signature,
        message,
        padding.PSS(
            mgf=padding.MGF1(hashes.SHA256()),
          salt_length=padding.PSS.MAX_LENGTH
        ),
        hashes.SHA256()
    )
    print("Signature verification successful. The message is authentic.")
except Exception as e:
    print("Signature verification failed. The message may have been tampered with or the
signature is invalid.")

# Tamper with the message to simulate alteration
tampered_message = b"Important message that has been altered."

# Attempt to verify the tampered message
try:
    public_key.verify(
        signature,
        tampered_message,
        padding.PSS(
            mgf=padding.MGF1(hashes.SHA256()),
            salt_length=padding.PSS.MAX_LENGTH
        ),
        hashes.SHA256()
    )
    print("Signature verification successful. The tampered message is authentic (which should
not happen).")
except Exception as e:
    print("Signature verification failed. The tampered message is not authentic.")
-----------------------------------------------------------------------------------------
```

Output:

```
Signature verification successful. The message is authentic.
Signature verification failed. The tampered message is not authentic.
```

Code Explanation:

Key Pair Generation:

- A key pair (private_key and public_key) is generated using RSA encryption with a key size of 2048 bits. The private key is used for signing, and the public key is used for verification.

Signing:

- private_key.sign() signs the message with the sender's private key using the PSS (Probabilistic Signature Scheme) padding and SHA-256 hashing algorithm.

Verification:

- public_key.verify() verifies the signature against the message using the sender's public key, ensuring that the message has not been altered and is authentic.

Tampering Simulation:

- To demonstrate the importance of digital signatures, tampered_message is altered. When verified with the original signature, verification fails, indicating tampering.

Digital signatures are essential in cybersecurity for ensuring data integrity, authentication, and non-repudiation in various applications such as electronic transactions, secure document exchange, and software distribution. They provide a robust mechanism to detect any unauthorized modifications to data and verify its origin, maintaining trust and security in digital communications.

Notes:
Digital signatures and certificates also rely on the principles of asymmetric encryption, which involves a pair of keys: a private key and a public key.

How Digital Signatures and Certificates Use Private and Public Keys:

Private Key:

- A private key is kept secret and known only to the owner. It is used for generating digital signatures.

Public Key:

- A public key is distributed openly and used by others to verify digital signatures created with the corresponding private key.

Digital Signatures:
Signing:

- To create a digital signature, the sender uses their private key to encrypt a hash (digest) of the message. This encrypted hash serves as the signature.

Verification:

- The recipient uses the sender's public key to decrypt and verify the signature. If the decrypted hash matches the hash of the received message, the signature is valid and ensures that the message has not been altered and comes from the expected sender.

Certificates:
Role:

- Certificates act as digital identities and contain information about the owner, the public key, and the certificate's validity period.

Issuance:

- Certificates are issued by trusted third parties known as Certificate Authorities (CAs). CAs digitally sign certificates with their private keys to attest to the authenticity of the certificate's contents.

Verification:

- When someone receives a certificate, they can verify its authenticity using the CA's public key. This process ensures that the certificate holder is who they claim to be and that the public key contained within the certificate is valid and trustworthy.

Digital signatures and certificates leverage the security provided by asymmetric encryption. Private keys are used for signing messages or documents, while public keys are used for verifying signatures and validating certificates. This cryptographic framework ensures data integrity, authenticity, and non-repudiation in digital communications, underpinning the security of transactions, communications, and sensitive information exchanges in modern cybersecurity practices.

Chapter 6

Identity and Access Management

Learning Outcomes:

Upon completing this chapter, you will be able to:

- *Understand the fundamental concepts of IAM and its importance in cybersecurity.*
- *Explore various authentication methods including passwords, biometrics, and multi-factor authentication (MFA).*
- *Discuss authorization mechanisms and access control models, including role-based and attribute-based access.*
- *Learn about identity management solutions such as Single Sign-On (SSO), Federated Identity Management (FIM), and Identity as a Service (IDaaS).*
- *Implement best practices to enhance IAM security and compliance in organizations.*

6.1 Authentication Methods

Authentication is the process of verifying the identity of users or systems before granting access to resources, such as networks, applications, or data. It is a crucial component of security, ensuring that only legitimate users can access restricted systems.

Passwords

Passwords are the most widely used authentication method. They are secret strings of characters that users provide to verify their identity. However, while still common, passwords alone are increasingly viewed as insufficient due to security risks associated with weak or reused passwords.

Best Practices:

Complexity: Strong passwords should combine upper and lowercase letters, numbers, and special characters.

Length: Longer passwords (8-12 characters or more) offer greater protection against brute force attacks.

Regular Updates: Users should change their passwords periodically to minimize exposure to breaches.

Avoid Reuse: Passwords should be unique across different accounts to limit the risk of compromised credentials affecting multiple systems.

Password Managers: Tools that generate and store complex passwords securely can significantly enhance password management.

Biometrics

Biometric authentication relies on unique biological traits for identity verification. This method is gaining popularity due to its security and convenience. Common biometric methods include fingerprint scanning, facial recognition, iris and retina scans, and voice recognition.

Types:

Fingerprint Scanning: Verifies users based on their fingerprint patterns.
Facial Recognition: Authenticates users by analyzing their facial features.
Iris and Retina Scanning: Uses detailed patterns of the iris or retina for identity verification.
Voice Recognition: Identifies users based on their unique voice patterns.

Benefits:

Security: Biometric traits are difficult to replicate or forge.
Convenience: Users do not need to remember passwords, enhancing ease of use.

Multi-Factor Authentication (MFA)

MFA adds additional layers of security by requiring users to provide two or more types of authentication. This method combines multiple factors to increase protection, making it much harder for attackers to gain unauthorized access.

Factors in MFA:

Something You Know: A password, PIN, or secret answer.
Something You Have: A physical device such as a smart card, token, or mobile device.
Something You Are: Biometric traits, such as a fingerprint or voice.

Implementation:

One-Time Passwords (OTPs): Temporary codes sent via SMS or email.
Authenticator Apps: Time-based OTPs generated by apps like Google Authenticator.
Hardware Tokens: Devices that generate secure, time-limited passwords.

Benefits:

Enhanced Security: MFA significantly reduces the risk of unauthorized access by requiring multiple proofs of identity.
Compliance: Meets regulatory requirements for securing sensitive data, particularly in industries like finance and healthcare.

6.2 Authorization and Access Control

Once a user's identity is authenticated, authorization determines the resources and actions the user is permitted to access. It enforces security policies to ensure users can only perform actions they are authorized to.

Authorization defines the permissions and access rights granted to users based on their roles or specific attributes. It ensures that even after authentication, users can only access data or resources for which they have been authorized.

Access Control is the mechanism that enforces these policies, restricting or allowing access to resources such as files, applications, or network services.

Models of Access Control:
Discretionary Access Control (DAC): Resource owners set permissions for who can access their data.

Mandatory Access Control (MAC): A central authority enforces strict policies, often used in military and government systems.

Role-Based Access Control (RBAC): Users are assigned predefined roles, and access is granted based on the role they hold. Commonly used in corporate environments to manage user permissions efficiently.

Attribute-Based Access Control (ABAC): Access is granted based on attributes of the user, such as their department, job title, or security clearance. This model is more dynamic than RBAC.

Implementation Tools:
Access Control Lists (ACLs): Define who has permission to access specific resources.

Policies: Define what actions users can perform on the system.

Permissions Management: Ensures users have only the necessary permissions to perform their tasks, following the principle of least privilege, which limits access to the minimum required for operational tasks.

Visual 6.1 illustrates security and authentication methods.

Visual 6:1: Security and Authentication

6.3 Identity Management Solutions

Identity Management (IdM) involves processes and technologies that manage digital identities and control user access throughout the identity lifecycle, from creation to deletion.

Key Components:
Identity Lifecycle Management: Manages every stage of the user's identity from onboarding to deactivation.

Directory Services: Central repositories like LDAP and Active Directory store identity data and provide identity-based services.

Provisioning and Deprovisioning: Automates the process of assigning and revoking user access based on role changes or terminations.

Self-Service Portals: Allow users to manage their profiles, change passwords, and request access without needing IT intervention.

Single Sign-On (SSO)
SSO simplifies user authentication by allowing them to access multiple applications or systems with a single login. This reduces password fatigue and improves security by centralizing authentication.

Benefits:
Convenience: Users no longer need to manage multiple passwords.
Security: Reduces the risk of weak or reused passwords across different systems.

Federated Identity Management (FIM)
FIM extends the SSO concept across multiple organizations or domains. It enables users to authenticate once and access resources in different organizations without needing multiple identities.

Standards Used in FIM:
SAML (Security Assertion Markup Language): An XML-based framework for exchanging authentication and authorization data.

OAuth: A protocol that allows secure authorization without sharing passwords.

OpenID Connect: An authentication layer built on top of OAuth 2.0 that provides SSO across different domains.

Identity Governance and Administration (IGA)
IGA ensures that identity management policies are enforced, especially in terms of access control and compliance with legal requirements.

Key Components:
Access Reviews: Periodic checks to ensure users have the appropriate level of access.

Role Management: Assigning roles to users and managing their permissions.

Compliance Reporting: Audits of identity and access management activities to ensure compliance with regulations.

Identity as a Service (IDaaS)
IDaaS provides identity management solutions via the cloud, offering scalable and cost-effective identity services to organizations. This allows businesses to manage digital identities without maintaining extensive on-premises infrastructure.

Benefits:
Scalability: Grows with organizational needs, providing flexibility in managing identities.
Cost-Effectiveness: Reduces the need for on-premises identity management solutions.
Integration: Seamlessly integrates with cloud applications and services.

6.4 Summary

This chapter explored the vital role of Identity and Access Management (IAM) in securing systems and data. It introduced different authentication methods, including passwords, biometrics, and multi-factor authentication (MFA), and discussed authorization mechanisms and access control models like DAC, MAC, RBAC, and ABAC. Identity management solutions, including SSO, FIM, and IDaaS, were also examined, highlighting their role in simplifying user access and maintaining security. By implementing robust IAM practices, organizations can enhance security, ensure compliance, and protect sensitive resources from unauthorized access.

Exercise 6

1. Discussion: Compare and contrast password-based authentication with biometric authentication. Discuss the advantages and disadvantages of each method.

2. Scenario Analysis: Design an access control policy for a financial institution. Consider roles, permissions, and regulatory compliance.

3. Case Study: Research and present a case study of an organization implementing Single Sign-On (SSO) for their enterprise systems. Analyze the benefits achieved and challenges faced.

4. Critical Thinking: Debate the effectiveness of multi-factor authentication (MFA) in preventing unauthorized access compared to traditional password-based authentication.

Example Python Code for Identity and Access Management (IAM)

Context:

This example demonstrates a Role-Based Access Control (RBAC) system enhanced with Multi-Factor Authentication (MFA). RBAC restricts user access to resources based on roles, ensuring that only users with the necessary permissions can access specific functionalities. Adding an MFA layer increases security by requiring an additional verification step, reducing the risk of unauthorized access, even if login credentials are compromised.

Usefulness:

- *Access Control: Ensures users access only the resources their role permits, protecting sensitive information and critical functions.*
- *Enhanced Security: MFA adds a second layer of security, safeguarding against unauthorized access due to compromised passwords.*
- *User Verification: The MFA code ensures that the person attempting access is the legitimate user, especially useful in high-security applications.*

Input Features:

- *Username: Identifies the user logging into the system.*
- *Password: Authenticates the user's identity as part of the initial login process.*
- *Role: Specifies the access level (e.g., admin, user, guest), determining which resources the user can access.*
- *MFA Code: A unique code sent to the user for verification, required to complete the login process.*

Code:

```
import random

# Sample users database
users_db = {
    "admin_user": {"password": "adminpass", "role": "admin"},
    "normal_user": {"password": "userpass", "role": "user"},
    "guest_user": {"password": "guestpass", "role": "guest"}
}

# Resource access control based on roles
role_permissions = {
    "admin": ["read", "write", "delete"],
    "user": ["read", "write"],
    "guest": ["read"]
}

# Function for multi-factor authentication (MFA)
def send_mfa_code():
    # Generate a random 6-digit MFA code
    return random.randint(100000, 999999)

def login(username, password):
    if username in users_db and users_db[username]["password"] == password:
        print(f"Login successful for {username}")
        role = users_db[username]["role"]
        print(f"Assigned role: {role}")
```

```
        # MFA verification
        mfa_code = send_mfa_code()
        print(f"MFA Code sent: {mfa_code}")

        entered_code = int(input("Enter the MFA code: "))
        if entered_code == mfa_code:
            print("MFA verification successful!")
            return role
        else:
            print("MFA verification failed!")
            return None
    else:
        print("Invalid username or password.")
        return None

# Function to check resource access based on role
def check_access(role, action):
    if role in role_permissions and action in role_permissions[role]:
        print(f"Access granted to perform '{action}' action.")
    else:
        print(f"Access denied for '{action}' action.")

# Simulation
username = input("Enter username: ")
password = input("Enter password: ")

# Login and MFA step
role = login(username, password)

if role:
    # Check if user has access to certain actions
    action = input("Enter the action you want to perform (read/write/delete): ")
    check_access(role, action)
```

Sample run:

```
Enter username: admin_user
Enter password: adminpass
Login successful for admin_user
Assigned role: admin
MFA Code sent: 345678
Enter the MFA code: 345678
MFA verification successful!
Enter the action you want to perform (read/write/delete): delete
Access granted to perform 'delete' action.
```

Code Explanation:

User Database: The users_db dictionary stores users, their passwords, and roles (e.g., admin, user, guest).

Role Permissions: The role_permissions dictionary defines what actions each role is allowed to perform (e.g., admin can read, write, delete, while a guest can only read).

MFA Process: After a successful password check, an MFA code is generated using send_mfa_code(), and the user is asked to enter it for verification.

Login: The login() function handles the username and password check. If the MFA step is successful, it returns the user's role.

Access Control: The check_access() function checks if the user's role has the necessary permissions to perform a specific action (read, write, delete).

Results:

- Successful Login + MFA: If the username/password combination and MFA verification succeed, the user can attempt actions based on their role.
- Access Control: The user is either granted or denied access based on their role and the requested action.

Chapter 7
Incident Response and Management

Learning Outcomes:

Upon completing this chapter, you will be able to:

- *Understand the key components of an Incident Response Plan (IRP) and their critical role in protecting organizational assets and data during a cyber incident.*
- *Identify the sequential steps involved in responding to a cyber incident, from preparation to recovery and post-incident review.*
- *Recognize the roles and responsibilities of an Incident Response Team (IRT) and their coordination in managing incidents.*
- *Describe the digital forensics process, including evidence collection, analysis, and reporting, and understand the importance of the chain of custody in handling digital evidence.*
- *Discuss strategies for continuous improvement in incident response by learning from past incidents.*

7.1 Incident Response Plan

An Incident Response Plan (IRP) is a structured framework that outlines the approach an organization takes to address and manage the aftermath of a security breach or cyber incident. Its goal is to mitigate damage, limit recovery time and costs, and ensure that key stakeholders are informed.

Key Components of an IRP:

Incident Definition: Clearly define what constitutes an incident, including security breaches, malware infections, unauthorized access, or denial-of-service attacks.

Roles and Responsibilities: Assign specific roles within the Incident Response Team (IRT) to manage different aspects of the incident. This ensures that every member of the team knows their responsibilities during an incident.

Communication Plan: Establish protocols for communicating internally and externally during an incident. It includes when to escalate the issue to higher management, when to inform affected stakeholders, and how to report to regulatory bodies if required.

Detection and Reporting: Set up systems and processes for detecting potential incidents. Reporting mechanisms should be in place for employees to report suspicious activity.

Containment and Mitigation: Outline procedures to isolate the affected systems or networks to prevent further damage. Implement strategies to mitigate the incident's impact while maintaining business continuity.

Eradication and Recovery: Detail steps to remove the threat, such as deleting malicious software, disabling compromised accounts, and patching vulnerabilities. After eradication, restore affected systems to full operational status.

Post-Incident Analysis: Conduct a review of the incident to understand its root cause, evaluate the effectiveness of the response, and identify improvements to be made to policies and procedures.

Documentation: Throughout the response process, it is crucial to document every action taken, including who performed it, when, and why. This documentation is important for audits, legal purposes, and future learning.

Visual 7:1 illustrates security incidence response lifecycle.

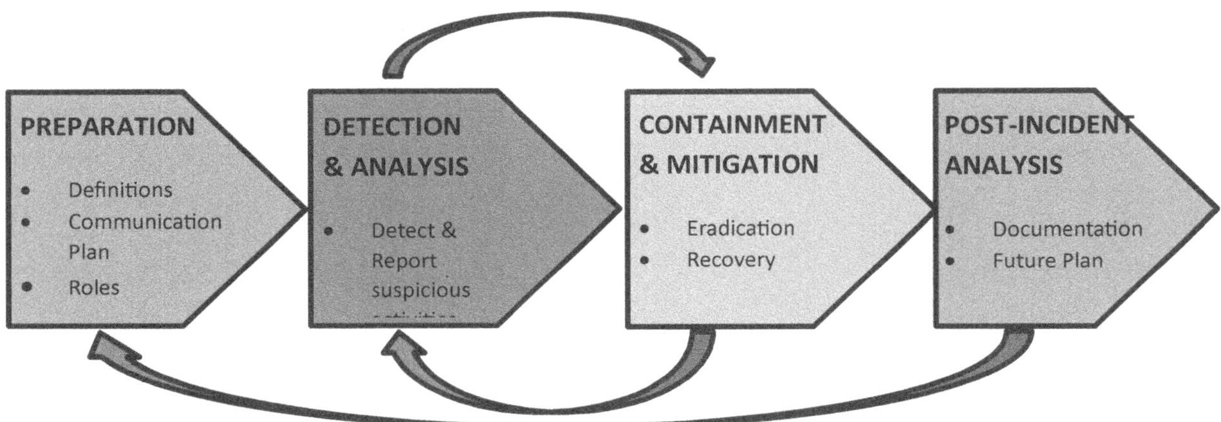

Visual 7.1: Incident Response Lifecycle

7.2 Steps in Responding to a Cyber Incident

Effective incident response requires a series of well-coordinated steps to identify, contain, and mitigate the impact of an incident while ensuring a swift recovery.

Preparation:

Review the IRP: Regularly update and review the Incident Response Plan to ensure it remains relevant and effective. Ensure that all personnel are familiar with their roles and the processes.

Training and Drills: Conduct regular training sessions and simulated drills to prepare the response team and other staff for potential cyber incidents. This helps identify weaknesses and ensures everyone is prepared.

Identification:
Detecting Incidents: Use monitoring tools such as intrusion detection systems (IDS), firewalls, and security information and event management (SIEM) systems to identify suspicious activity that may indicate a security breach.

Incident Reporting: Encourage employees to report any unusual activity immediately. Early detection is key to minimizing damage.

Containment:
Short-Term Containment: Immediately isolate compromised systems to prevent the threat from spreading to other parts of the network.

Long-Term Containment: Implement additional protective measures, such as deploying patches or updates, while continuing normal business operations to avoid further compromise.

Eradication:
Remove the Threat: Ensure that all traces of the malicious code or unauthorized access are removed. This includes deleting malware, disabling affected accounts, and eliminating any backdoors or vulnerabilities.

Patch and Update: Apply necessary patches to fix the exploited vulnerabilities and ensure that the systems are secured to prevent recurrence.

Recovery:
Restore Systems: Once the threat is eradicated, restore the affected systems and data from backups if necessary. Ensure that recovery does not inadvertently reintroduce the threat.

Validate Recovery: Test systems and applications to ensure they are fully functional and free from vulnerabilities.

Lessons Learned:
Post-Incident Review: Conduct a thorough review of the incident to identify areas for improvement. The review should assess what went well, what did not, and how the process can be improved.

Documentation and Reporting: Document all actions taken during the response, lessons learned, and recommended improvements to policies, procedures, and tools.

7.3 Roles and Responsibilities in Incident Response

An effective incident response requires a well-organized team with clearly defined roles. The Incident Response Team (IRT) should include members from various parts of the organization, each with specific responsibilities.

Key Roles in the IRT:

Incident Manager: Responsible for overall coordination and management of the incident response process. They ensure that communication between team members is clear and that the response is progressing effectively.

Technical Lead: Oversees the technical aspects of the response, including identifying and mitigating the threat. They work closely with the security team to implement containment, eradication, and recovery strategies.

Forensic Analyst: Collects and analyzes evidence from compromised systems to determine the nature and extent of the attack. They ensure that all digital evidence is preserved and documented for future investigation or legal action.

Communications Coordinator: Manages communication with internal and external stakeholders, ensuring that the right information is shared at the right time.

Legal Counsel: Provides advice on legal and regulatory matters, including compliance with data breach notification laws and potential liability.

Public Relations: Handles communication with the media and the public to manage the organization's reputation during and after the incident.

Executive Leadership: Senior management provides decision-making authority and allocates resources to support the response effort.

7.4 Forensics and Analysis

Digital Forensics is a critical part of incident response. It involves the collection, preservation, analysis, and reporting of digital evidence to understand the full scope of the incident and to aid in legal proceedings if necessary.

Digital Forensics Process:

Evidence Collection: Securely collect relevant digital evidence, such as logs, network traffic data, and system images. It is important to preserve this evidence in a way that maintains its integrity.

Documentation: Maintain a chain of custody to document who has handled the evidence, when, and for what purpose. This ensures that the evidence remains admissible in court if needed.

Analysis: Analyze the evidence to identify how the attack occurred, what systems were affected, and the techniques used by the attackers. Memory forensics and network analysis tools are often used at this stage.

Reporting: Prepare a detailed report on the findings, including recommendations for strengthening defenses to prevent similar attacks in the future.

Tools and Techniques:

Data Acquisition Tools: Used to capture forensic images of hard drives, memory, and other storage media.

Network Analysis Tools: Monitor network traffic to detect anomalies and suspicious activity.

Memory Forensics: Involves examining volatile memory (RAM) to uncover malware or traces of the attacker's activities.

File Integrity Checking: Ensures that files have not been altered by comparing their current state with known good versions.

Chain of Custody is essential in forensics. It ensures that evidence is preserved securely, properly documented, and authenticated to prevent tampering or loss.

Before concluding this chapter, it is helpful to explore additional resources that can assist cybersecurity professionals and incident responders during investigations. Four appendices are provided at the end of this book to serve as quick references:

- **Appendix A** lists essential tools commonly used by investigators for various tasks such as network analysis, vulnerability scanning, and forensic investigation.
- **Appendix B** introduces the MITRE ATT&CK Framework, a valuable resource for mapping attacker tactics, techniques, and procedures (TTPs), enabling responders to understand attack patterns and improve detection and response.
- **Appendix C** presents useful Windows commands for analyzing processes, services, users, and event logs during investigations.
- **Appendix D** offers a collection of Linux commands that aid in monitoring, scanning, and forensic analysis within Linux-based environments.

These appendices aim to enhance the practical application of incident response concepts covered in this chapter.

7.5 Summary

This chapter covered the critical components of incident response and management. By following a structured Incident Response Plan, organizations can efficiently detect, contain, and mitigate cyber incidents. Key steps in responding to incidents include preparation, identification, containment, eradication, and recovery. We also explored the importance of digital forensics in analyzing incidents and preserving evidence for legal and operational purposes. Effective incident response not only minimizes the damage caused by cyber attacks but also provides valuable insights to strengthen security defenses for the future.

Exercise 7

1. Scenario Analysis: Develop hypothetical scenarios of different cyber incidents (e.g., ransomware attack, data breach) and outline how each incident would be handled according to the Incident Response Plan.

2. Role Play Exercise: Assign roles within a simulated incident scenario and practice communication, decision-making, and coordination among team members.

3. IRP Evaluation: Review and critique an existing Incident Response Plan from a real-world case study, identifying strengths, weaknesses, and areas for improvement.

4. Forensic Investigation Practice: Conduct a mock digital forensic investigation using sample data to practice evidence collection, analysis, and reporting.

Example Python Code for Incident Response Plan (IRP)

Context:

This example demonstrates a simulated incident response workflow for handling detected cyber threats. Upon identifying suspicious network activity, the response team follows a structured approach with key phases: Detection, Containment, Eradication, Recovery, and Post-Incident Review. This incident response process helps manage and mitigate potential threats effectively, reducing downtime and minimizing the impact on the system.

Usefulness:

- Structured Response: Provides a systematic approach to handling incidents, ensuring that all necessary steps are completed.
- Threat Mitigation: Quickly contains and eradicates threats to minimize damage.
- Continuous Improvement: The Post-Incident Review identifies lessons learned, enabling improved response strategies for future incidents.

Input Features:

- Incident Type: Specifies the nature of the detected threat (e.g., malware, unauthorized access).
- System Status: Indicates whether the system is currently operating normally or compromised.
- Containment Strategy: Outlines the chosen method to isolate and limit the spread of the threat.
- Eradication Plan: Details the steps taken to completely remove the threat from the system.
- Recovery Actions: Describes the actions required to restore systems to their normal, operational state.

Code:

```
import random

# Step 1: Incident Detection
def detect_incident():
    incident_types = ["Malware", "Unauthorized Access", "DDoS Attack", "Phishing"]
    incident_detected = random.choice(incident_types)
    print(f"Incident Detected: {incident_detected}")
    return incident_detected

# Step 2: Containment
def contain_incident(incident_type):
    print(f"Containment Strategy for {incident_type}:")
    if incident_type == "Malware":
        print("Isolating infected system from the network.")
    elif incident_type == "Unauthorized Access":
        print("Disabling compromised user accounts.")
    elif incident_type == "DDoS Attack":
        print("Activating DDoS mitigation services.")
    elif incident_type == "Phishing":
        print("Blocking malicious emails and alerting users.")
    print("Incident contained.")
```

```
# Step 3: Eradication
def eradicate_incident(incident_type):
    print(f"Eradication Plan for {incident_type}:")
    if incident_type == "Malware":
        print("Running antivirus scan and removing malware.")
    elif incident_type == "Unauthorized Access":
        print("Reviewing access logs and removing unauthorized users.")
    elif incident_type == "DDoS Attack":
        print("Blocking malicious IPs and restoring traffic flow.")
    elif incident_type == "Phishing":


        print("Removing phishing emails from user inboxes.")
    print("Threat eradicated.")

# Step 4: Recovery
def recover_system():
    print("Restoring systems to normal operation.")
    print("Recovering data from backups and applying security patches.")
    print("System successfully recovered.")

# Step 5: Post-Incident Review
def post_incident_review(incident_type):
    print(f"Post-Incident Review for {incident_type}:")
    print("Analyzing logs and performance metrics.")
    print("Evaluating response time and effectiveness.")
    print("Identifying areas for improvement in the Incident Response Plan.")
    print("Post-incident review completed.")

# Simulating the Incident Response Lifecycle
incident = detect_incident()

contain_incident(incident)
eradicate_incident(incident)
recover_system()
post_incident_review(incident)
```

Example run:

```
Incident Detected: Malware
Containment Strategy for Malware:
Isolating infected system from the network.
Incident contained.
Eradication Plan for Malware:
Running antivirus scan and removing malware.
Threat eradicated.
Restoring systems to normal operation.
Recovering data from backups and applying security patches.
System successfully recovered.
Post-Incident Review for Malware:
Analyzing logs and performance metrics.
Evaluating response time and effectiveness.
Identifying areas for improvement in the Incident Response Plan.
Post-incident review completed.
```

Code Explanation:

Incident Detection: The function detect_incident() simulates the detection of a cyber incident by randomly selecting an incident type (e.g., malware, phishing, unauthorized access). This represents the initial step in incident response.

Containment: Once an incident is detected, the contain_incident() function initiates an appropriate containment strategy to prevent the threat from spreading (e.g., isolating infected systems).

Eradication: The eradicate_incident() function describes the steps taken to remove the threat from the system, such as removing malware or disabling compromised accounts.

Recovery: The recover_system() function focuses on restoring the system to its normal state by recovering data from backups and ensuring that the security patches are applied.

Post-Incident Review: The post_incident_review() function represents the final phase of incident response, where the team evaluates the effectiveness of their response and identifies areas for improvement.

Results:

- The code simulates an entire incident response lifecycle, showing how an organization might detect, contain, eradicate, recover, and learn from an incident.
- For each incident type, a specific containment and eradication strategy is applied, and a post-incident review ensures continuous improvement in response efforts.

This Python example demonstrates the flow of an incident response plan, reflecting the real-world process of responding to cyber incidents. It highlights the importance of having structured response steps to minimize the impact of incidents and ensure quick recovery.

Chapter 8

Data Protection and Privacy

Learning Outcomes:

Upon completing this chapter, you will be able to:

- *Understand the importance of data classification and its role in data protection strategies.*
- *Describe best practices for data handling, including access control, encryption, and secure disposal.*
- *Recognize different levels of data sensitivity and apply appropriate handling guidelines.*
- *Explain data masking and encryption techniques for protecting sensitive information.*
- *Discuss key regulatory compliance requirements such as GDPR and HIPAA.*
- *Identify strategies for implementing compliance measures, including data governance and privacy impact assessments.*

8.1 Data Classification and Handling

Data Classification

Data classification is the systematic process of organizing data into categories based on its sensitivity, value, or regulatory requirements. The primary purpose is to determine the level of security controls needed to protect the data throughout its lifecycle, from creation to disposal. This approach ensures that sensitive data receives the appropriate protection, reducing the risk of unauthorized access, theft, or misuse.

Levels of Classification:

Public Data: Information that can be freely shared without any risk to the organization. Examples include publicly available reports or marketing materials.

Internal Data: Restricted to employees within the organization and not intended for public disclosure, such as internal memos and operational procedures.

Confidential Data: Sensitive information requiring strict access controls, including financial records, intellectual property, and personally identifiable information (PII).

Classification Methods:
Automated Classification: Software tools automatically classify data based on predefined rules, ensuring consistency and efficiency across the organization. Automated tools reduce the likelihood of human error.

Manual Classification: Employees manually assign classification labels to data, which is often necessary for nuanced or context-specific data, such as legal documents or proprietary information.

Data Handling Practices
Proper data handling is critical to maintaining the confidentiality, integrity, and availability of data. Different classification levels demand varying degrees of security measures.

Key Practices:
Access Control: Restrict access based on the classification of the data. Role-based access control (RBAC) and multi-factor authentication (MFA) are widely used to ensure that only authorized personnel can access sensitive data.

Encryption: Encrypting data both in transit and at rest is essential to prevent unauthorized access or interception. Strong encryption algorithms and proper key management are required to protect sensitive information.

Retention Policies: Clearly defined retention policies help determine how long data should be kept based on business needs and legal requirements. Data should be securely deleted when it is no longer required.

Data Minimization: Collect only the necessary data for legitimate business purposes, limiting the exposure in the event of a data breach. This principle also helps comply with data privacy regulations.

Secure Disposal: Proper disposal methods, such as shredding paper documents and securely erasing digital files, ensure that data is rendered irrecoverable once it is no longer needed.

8.2 Data Sensitivity Levels

Understanding and applying appropriate data sensitivity levels allows organizations to implement the right security controls for different types of data. This section explores the common sensitivity levels and their associated security measures.

Levels of Sensitivity:
Public Data: Intended for public consumption, such as marketing brochures or press releases. This data requires minimal protection.

Internal Data: Internal business information that is restricted to employees or authorized personnel but not classified as sensitive.

Sensitive Data: Information requiring special handling, such as PII, financial records, or healthcare data. Unauthorized access could lead to legal, financial, or reputational damage.

Highly Confidential Data: The most critical information to the organization, including trade secrets, strategic business plans, and proprietary algorithms. This data requires the highest levels of protection and access restrictions.

Handling Guidelines:
Access Controls: Stringent access controls, including role-based and attribute-based access control, ensure that only authorized personnel can access sensitive or highly confidential data.

Encryption: Sensitive data should always be encrypted during storage and transmission. Modern encryption algorithms, such as AES-256, provide strong protection against unauthorized access.

Monitoring and Auditing: Regularly monitor access to sensitive data, and perform audits to ensure that security measures are being followed. Automated alerts can notify administrators of unauthorized access attempts or suspicious activity.

8.3 Data Masking and Encryption

Data Masking

Data masking is a technique used to protect sensitive information by replacing it with fictitious, yet realistic data, making it unreadable to unauthorized users. This is commonly used in non-production environments, such as development and testing, where access to real data is unnecessary.

Types of Data Masking:
Static Masking: Permanently alters sensitive data before it is transferred to a non-production environment. This method ensures that sensitive information is never exposed outside secure environments.

Dynamic Masking: Temporarily masks data in real-time, ensuring that sensitive information is protected when accessed by unauthorized users. Dynamic masking is often used for role-based access within live systems.

Use Cases: Data masking is valuable in scenarios where sensitive data needs to be used for analytics, testing, or research without compromising its confidentiality. For example, masking customer information in a development environment prevents exposure of real data while allowing developers to test functionalities.

Encryption

Encryption is the process of converting readable data into an unreadable format (ciphertext) using cryptographic algorithms. Only those with the correct decryption key can convert the ciphertext back to its original form (plaintext), ensuring that sensitive data is protected even if intercepted.

Types of Encryption:
In Transit: SSL/TLS encryption is used to protect data moving between systems, such as web traffic or email communications.

At Rest: Encrypting stored data ensures that sensitive information, such as database records or files on a server, remains secure even if the storage device is compromised.

Key Management: Effective key management is critical to ensuring the security of encrypted data. Keys must be securely stored and regularly rotated to prevent unauthorized access.

8.4 Regulatory Compliance

GDPR (General Data Protection Regulation)
GDPR is a comprehensive data privacy regulation that applies to any organization processing personal data of individuals residing in the EU, regardless of the organization's location.

Key Provisions:
Data Subject Rights: Individuals have rights to access, correct, or delete their personal data, and organizations must comply within specified timeframes.

Data Breach Notification: Organizations must notify the relevant authorities within 72 hours of discovering a data breach and inform affected individuals if their rights are at risk.

Penalties: Non-compliance can result in significant fines of up to €20 million or 4% of annual global turnover, whichever is higher.

HIPAA (Health Insurance Portability and Accountability Act)
HIPAA is a US law designed to protect sensitive patient health information, establishing strict standards for healthcare organizations and their business associates.

Key Requirements:
Protected Health Information (PHI): PHI includes medical records, billing information, and any individually identifiable health information. HIPAA mandates specific safeguards to protect PHI.

Administrative, Physical, and Technical Safeguards: These include ensuring that only authorized individuals have access to PHI, securing physical locations where PHI is stored, and implementing encryption for electronic PHI.

8.5 Understanding Data Privacy Laws and Implementing Compliance Measures

Data Privacy Laws
Compliance with data privacy laws is critical for organizations handling personal or sensitive data. Laws such as GDPR, HIPAA, and CCPA (California Consumer Privacy Act) impose strict requirements on how organizations collect, store, and process personal data.

Key Compliance Strategies:
Data Governance: Implementing a robust data governance framework helps organizations manage data effectively and ensure compliance with privacy laws.

Privacy Impact Assessments (PIAs): Conducting PIAs allows organizations to assess and mitigate privacy risks associated with new projects or data processing activities.

Training and Awareness: Educating employees on data protection policies, privacy laws, and security best practices is essential for maintaining compliance and protecting sensitive information.

Auditing and Monitoring: Regular audits and continuous monitoring help identify potential compliance issues and ensure that data handling practices align with regulatory requirements.

Visual 8:1 illustrates data protection and privacy dimensions.

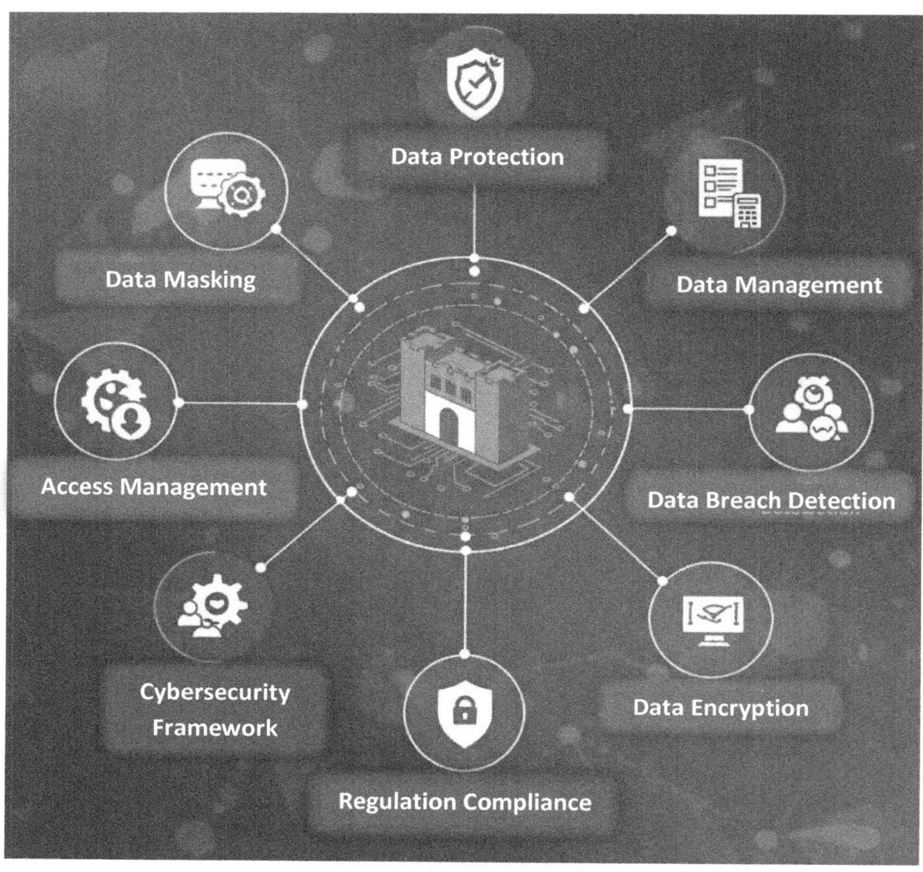

Visual 8:1 Data Protection and Privacy

Visual 8:2 illustrates data protection and privacy laws.

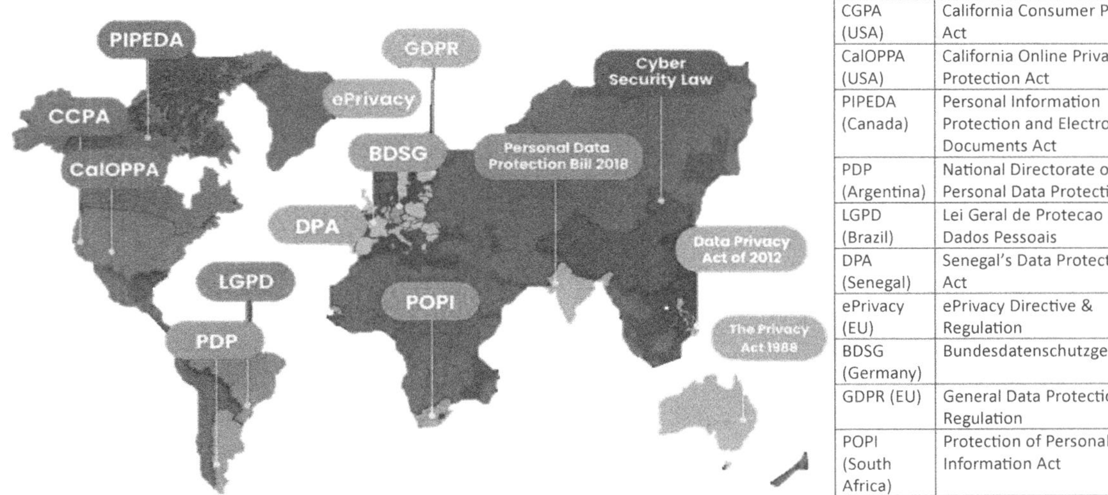

CGPA (USA)	California Consumer Privacy Act
CalOPPA (USA)	California Online Privacy Protection Act
PIPEDA (Canada)	Personal Information Protection and Electronic Documents Act
PDP (Argentina)	National Directorate of Personal Data Protection
LGPD (Brazil)	Lei Geral de Protecao de Dados Pessoais
DPA (Senegal)	Senegal's Data Protection Act
ePrivacy (EU)	ePrivacy Directive & Regulation
BDSG (Germany)	Bundesdatenschutzgesetz
GDPR (EU)	General Data Protection Regulation
POPI (South Africa)	Protection of Personal Information Act

Visual 8:2 Some Data Protection and Privacy Laws Worldwide

8.6 Summary

In this chapter, we explored the importance of data protection and privacy, including the classification and handling of sensitive data, encryption, data masking, and compliance with key regulatory frameworks such as GDPR and HIPAA. By implementing effective data governance, privacy assessments, and security measures, organizations can ensure the confidentiality, integrity, and availability of sensitive information while maintaining compliance with global data protection laws.

Exercise 8

1. Data Classification Exercise: Classify different types of organizational data into appropriate categories (Public, Internal, Confidential).
2. Compliance Scenario Analysis: Analyze a hypothetical scenario for GDPR or HIPAA compliance, identifying key requirements and potential impacts.
3. Data Handling Audit: Evaluate data handling practices within an organization, assessing access controls, encryption measures, and compliance with data retention policies.
4. Privacy Impact Assessment (PIA) Preparation: Draft a Privacy Impact Assessment (PIA) for a new data processing activity, identifying privacy risks and proposing mitigation strategies.

Example Python Code for
Data Encryption and Data Masking

Context:

This example demonstrates how to classify, encrypt, and mask sensitive customer information to enhance data security and regulatory compliance. The code showcases methods for securing data, ensuring that only authorized users can access full details, while masked or encrypted versions provide necessary information for analytics or reporting. This is crucial for protecting personal data and aligning with regulations such as GDPR and HIPAA.

Usefulness:

- Data Security: Protects sensitive data from unauthorized access through encryption and masking.
- Regulatory Compliance: Ensures that data handling aligns with legal standards, reducing the risk of non-compliance penalties.
- Controlled Data Access: Allows visibility for analytics without exposing full details, minimizing privacy risks.

Input Features:

- Data Classification: Categorizes data into levels (e.g., Public, Confidential) to determine the necessary security measures.
- Encryption: Encrypts critical information (e.g., personal identification numbers) to prevent unauthorized access.
- Data Masking: Masks sensitive data fields, partially hiding information for privacy while allowing limited analytics access.
- Compliance: Demonstrates adherence to data protection regulations by implementing secure data handling techniques.

Code:

```
from cryptography.fernet import Fernet
import pandas as pd

# Generate a key for encryption/decryption
# This key should be securely stored and managed
key = Fernet.generate_key()
cipher_suite = Fernet(key)

# Sample customer data
data = {
    'CustomerID': [1, 2, 3],
    'Name': ['Alice', 'Bob', 'Charlie'],
    'Email': ['alice@example.com', 'bob@example.com', 'charlie@example.com'],
    'SSN': ['123-45-6789', '987-65-4321', '456-78-9012']  # Social Security Numbers
(sensitive data)
}

# Convert the data into a pandas DataFrame
df = pd.DataFrame(data)

# Function to classify data
def classify_data(df):
    df['Classification'] = df['SSN'].apply(lambda x: 'Confidential' if x else 'Public')
    print("\nData Classification:")
    print(df[['CustomerID', 'Name', 'Classification']])
```

```
# Function to encrypt sensitive data
def encrypt_data(df):
    df['Encrypted_SSN'] = df['SSN'].apply(lambda x:
cipher_suite.encrypt(x.encode()).decode())
    print("\nEncrypted SSNs:")
    print(df[['CustomerID', 'Name', 'Encrypted_SSN']])

# Function to mask sensitive data
def mask_data(ssn):
    return ssn[:3] + '-XX-XXXX'

def apply_data_masking(df):
    df['Masked_SSN'] = df['SSN'].apply(mask_data)
    print("\nMasked SSNs:")
    print(df[['CustomerID', 'Name', 'Masked_SSN']])

# Step 1: Classify the data based on sensitivity
classify_data(df)

# Step 2: Encrypt sensitive data (Social Security Numbers)
encrypt_data(df)

# Step 3: Mask sensitive data for use in analytics (e.g., SSNs with some digits hidden)
apply_data_masking(df)

# Output showing compliance steps taken
print("\nData Protection Measures Applied: Data has been classified, encrypted, and masked to
ensure privacy and compliance with regulations.")
--------------------------------------------------------------------------------
```

```
Data Classification:
   CustomerID     Name Classification
0           1    Alice   Confidential
1           2      Bob   Confidential
2           3  Charlie   Confidential

Encrypted SSNs:
   CustomerID     Name                                      Encrypted_SSN
0           1    Alice  gAAAAABh8fGjJ7MlLzQzR5JbX7LOxMd5xwleM...
1           2      Bob  gAAAAABh8fGjdD3JnzmPlnVoxMcXwa9fPTVdM...
2           3  Charlie  gAAAAABh8fGjyVLBHaTQ7FY5yRfyzef5NPMFb...

Masked SSNs:
   CustomerID     Name   Masked_SSN
0           1    Alice  123-XX-XXXX
1           2      Bob  987-XX-XXXX
2           3  Charlie  456-XX-XXXX

Data Protection Measures Applied: Data has been classified, encrypted, and masked to ensure
privacy and compliance with regulations.
```

Code Explanation:

Data Classification: The classify_data() function classifies data based on sensitivity (e.g., Social Security Numbers are classified as "Confidential").

Encryption: The encrypt_data() function encrypts the sensitive information (SSN) using the cryptography library. This ensures that even if unauthorized access occurs, the sensitive data remains unreadable without the correct decryption key.

Data Masking: The apply_data_masking() function masks part of the sensitive data (SSN), ensuring that certain digits are hidden (e.g., 123-XX-XXXX). This is useful for sharing data for analytics while maintaining data privacy.

Compliance: This example illustrates how organizations can apply encryption and masking techniques to protect sensitive information and ensure compliance with data protection regulations such as GDPR and HIPAA.

Summary:
The code demonstrates a data protection and privacy workflow:

- Data classification identifies sensitive data.
- Encryption protects sensitive information like SSNs from unauthorized access.
- Data masking ensures partial data visibility for non-sensitive uses (e.g., analytics) while hiding critical information.

This approach ensures compliance with data protection laws like GDPR and HIPAA, safeguarding sensitive information while still allowing for controlled data usage.

Chapter 9

Security Awareness and Training

Learning Outcomes:

Upon completing this chapter, you will be able to:

- *Understand the importance of cybersecurity awareness in organizational resilience.*
- *Learn the key elements of effective employee training programs in cybersecurity.*
- *Explore various methods for delivering cybersecurity training and awareness programs.*
- *Recognize the role of regular training, simulations, and fostering a strong security culture.*
- *Learn how to promote best practices and encourage the reporting of suspicious activities.*

9.1 Employee Training Programs

Employee training programs in cybersecurity are essential for educating staff on the potential risks posed by cyber threats and the steps they can take to mitigate them. These programs aim to equip employees with the knowledge to recognize security threats and the practical skills to respond effectively.

Key Elements:

Basic Security Principles: Employees need to understand fundamental cybersecurity concepts like password security, phishing awareness, and safe browsing habits. By learning how to create strong, complex passwords and recognize phishing emails or malicious websites, employees can help protect organizational data.

Role-Specific Training: Different roles within the organization face varying levels of cybersecurity risks. Tailoring training to specific job functions ensures that each employee understands the particular threats relevant to their position. For example, IT staff may require in-depth knowledge of network security, while executives need to understand the implications of high-level data breaches.

Incident Response Training: Employees must be educated on their role in the incident response process, including how to report incidents quickly and effectively. A clearly defined incident response process can make the difference in containing and mitigating security breaches.

Compliance Training: Employees should be aware of the regulatory requirements surrounding data protection and privacy, such as GDPR, HIPAA, or industry-specific regulations. Understanding these requirements ensures the organization remains compliant and avoids legal penalties.

9.2 Delivery Methods

There are several effective methods for delivering cybersecurity training and awareness programs. The choice of method depends on the organization's size, culture, and resources.

Online Courses and Modules: Interactive e-learning platforms can offer cybersecurity modules covering topics such as phishing, social engineering, and data protection. These platforms often include quizzes and assessments to reinforce learning.

In-Person Workshops: Hands-on, in-person workshops are valuable for delivering practical training. These sessions can include live demonstrations, group discussions, and real-world case studies that enhance understanding and foster active participation.

Simulations and Tabletop Exercises: Simulated cyber incidents help employees practice their response in real-time. Tabletop exercises, where employees walk through a hypothetical scenario, help test organizational preparedness and improve incident response protocols.

9.3 Importance of Cybersecurity Awareness

Cybersecurity awareness is crucial for building an organization's resilience to cyber threats. Educated employees are better equipped to recognize suspicious activities and prevent security breaches.

Benefits of Awareness:

Risk Mitigation: Trained employees can identify potential threats, reducing the likelihood of successful cyber-attacks. For example, recognizing phishing emails can prevent malware from entering the system.

Early Detection: Employees who are aware of potential cyber threats are more likely to detect and report them early. Early detection is essential for limiting the damage caused by cyber incidents.

Compliance: Awareness programs help ensure that employees comply with data protection laws and regulations, reducing the risk of non-compliance and associated penalties.

Cultural Shift: A culture of security awareness empowers employees at all levels to take responsibility for protecting the organization's data and systems.

9.4 Regular Training and Simulations

Continuous training is necessary to keep employees updated on the latest cybersecurity trends and threats.

Threat Landscape Updates: The cybersecurity landscape is constantly evolving. Regular updates on new vulnerabilities, attack techniques, and defenses are essential to keep employees informed.

Annual Training: Annual refresher courses ensure that employees remain vigilant and aware of current best practices. These sessions should address emerging threats and evolving cybersecurity standards.

Phishing Simulations: Regular phishing simulations help assess employees' susceptibility to social engineering attacks. These exercises can also be used to reinforce proper email handling techniques.

Tabletop Exercises: Running tabletop exercises simulating cyber incidents, such as ransomware attacks or data breaches, allows the organization to evaluate response readiness, refine communication channels, and improve coordination among team members.

9.5 Creating a Security Culture

Building a strong security culture requires active support from leadership and engagement from all employees. A security culture ensures that cybersecurity becomes a shared responsibility across the organization.

Characteristics of a Security Culture:

Leadership Support: Top management must demonstrate commitment to cybersecurity by allocating resources, endorsing training programs, and leading by example. When leadership takes cybersecurity seriously, employees are more likely to follow suit.

Employee Engagement: Security initiatives should encourage employees to actively participate and contribute ideas for improving the organization's cybersecurity posture. This fosters a collaborative environment where everyone feels responsible for security.

Open Communication: Establish clear channels for employees to report security incidents or concerns without fear of retaliation. Transparent communication and responsive action build trust and encourage proactive reporting.

Recognition and Rewards: Recognize and reward employees who follow best practices and contribute to improving organizational security. Acknowledging their efforts reinforces positive behavior and motivates others to do the same.

9.6 Encouraging Best Practices and Reporting Suspicious Activities

To maintain robust cybersecurity defenses, it is crucial to promote best practices across the organization and establish a reliable process for reporting suspicious activities.

Promoting Best Practices:

Password Security: Emphasize the importance of creating strong, unique passwords and implementing multi-factor authentication (MFA) to protect accounts from unauthorized access.

Safe Browsing: Train employees to recognize phishing sites and avoid malicious links. Encourage them to verify the authenticity of websites before entering sensitive information.

Data Handling: Ensure employees follow proper data handling procedures, including encryption, access control, and data minimization.

Device Security: Encourage employees to keep software up to date and install security patches promptly. Enable firewalls and antivirus software to safeguard devices from malware.

Reporting Suspicious Activities:

Clear Reporting Procedures: Ensure employees know how and where to report suspicious emails, security incidents, or unusual activity. A designated point of contact or incident response team should handle these reports promptly.

Non-Retaliation Policy: Employees should feel confident that reporting incidents will not result in negative consequences. Promote a culture of accountability and encourage proactive reporting.

9.7 Summary

This chapter emphasized the importance of security awareness and training in safeguarding organizational assets. By educating employees about cybersecurity best practices and promoting a security-conscious culture, organizations can mitigate risks and reduce the likelihood of cyber-attacks. Regular training, simulations, and open communication are essential components of a strong security posture.

Exercise 9

1. Scenario Analysis: Develop a tabletop exercise that simulates a cyber incident, outlining how employees should respond, report, and communicate during the incident.

2. Phishing Simulation: Design a phishing simulation to test employees' ability to recognize and report phishing emails. Analyze the results and suggest areas for improvement.

3. Role-Specific Training: Create role-specific training modules for different departments (e.g., IT, HR, finance). Tailor the content to address their unique cybersecurity challenges and responsibilities.

Example of Python Code for Security Awareness Training Simulation

Context:

The Python script demonstrates an interactive training tool aimed at enhancing employee awareness of phishing threats. This tool helps organizations educate employees on recognizing phishing emails by simulating real-world scenarios, allowing employees to practice identifying and responding to potential phishing attempts. The interactive feedback provides valuable insights to reinforce learning.

Usefulness:

- Phishing Awareness: Educates employees on identifying phishing characteristics, reducing the likelihood of security breaches.
- Hands-On Learning: Engages users in a practical exercise, reinforcing learning through real-time feedback.
- Security Culture: Supports a proactive security culture by training employees to recognize and report suspicious activities.

Input Features:

- Sample Emails: A collection of email examples, both phishing and legitimate, for employees to classify.
- User Interaction: Prompts employees to assess each email and label it as either phishing or legitimate.
- Feedback Mechanism: Provides feedback for each selection, explaining why an email may or may not be phishing, improving employee understanding.

Code:

```
# Sample training simulation for phishing awareness

# A set of example emails for training
emails = [
    {
        "subject": "Urgent: Verify your account details!",
        "content": "Dear user, your account will be suspended unless you verify your details.
Click here to confirm.",
        "is_phishing": True
    },
    {
        "subject": "Monthly Newsletter from HR",
        "content": "Hello! Here is your monthly newsletter with updates and company
announcements. Have a great day!",
        "is_phishing": False
    },
    {
        "subject": "Security Alert: Unauthorized login attempt detected",
        "content": "We detected an unauthorized login attempt on your account. Please reset
your password immediately by clicking this link.",
        "is_phishing": True
    },
    {
        "subject": "Meeting Reminder: Quarterly Update",
        "content": "Just a reminder about the quarterly update meeting scheduled for tomorrow
at 10 AM. Please confirm your attendance.",
        "is_phishing": False
    }
]
```

```
# Function to simulate phishing awareness quiz
def phishing_awareness_training():
    print("Welcome to the Phishing Awareness Training Simulation!\n")
    correct_answers = 0

    # Loop through the emails and ask the user to classify them
    for i, email in enumerate(emails, 1):
        print(f"Email {i}:")
        print(f"Subject: {email['subject']}")
        print(f"Content: {email['content']}")
        user_input = input("Is this email a phishing attempt? (yes/no): ").strip().lower()

        if (user_input == "yes" and email['is_phishing']) or (user_input == "no" and not
email['is_phishing']):
            print("Correct! This is the right classification.\n")
            correct_answers += 1
        else:
            print("Incorrect. Here's why:\n")
            if email['is_phishing']:
                print("This email is a phishing attempt. Look for red flags like urgent
requests and suspicious links.\n")
            else:
                print("This email is legitimate. It contains no suspicious elements and comes
from a trusted source.\n")

    # Feedback on the user's performance
    print(f"Training complete! You got {correct_answers} out of {len(emails)} correct.")

# Run the phishing awareness training simulation
phishing_awareness_training()
-----------------------------------------------------------------------------------
Sample run:
Welcome to the Phishing Awareness Training Simulation!

Email 1:
Subject: Urgent: Verify your account details!
Content: Dear user, your account will be suspended unless you verify your details. Click here
to confirm.
Is this email a phishing attempt? (yes/no): yes
Correct! This is the right classification.

Email 2:
Subject: Monthly Newsletter from HR
Content: Hello! Here is your monthly newsletter with updates and company announcements. Have
a great day!
Is this email a phishing attempt? (yes/no): no
Correct! This is the right classification.

Email 3:
Subject: Security Alert: Unauthorized login attempt detected
Content: We detected an unauthorized login attempt on your account. Please reset your
password immediately by clicking this link.
Is this email a phishing attempt? (yes/no): yes
Correct! This is the right classification.
```

```
Email 4:
Subject: Meeting Reminder: Quarterly Update
Content: Just a reminder about the quarterly update meeting scheduled for tomorrow at 10 AM.
Please confirm your attendance.
Is this email a phishing attempt? (yes/no): no
Correct! This is the right classification.
Training complete! You got 4 out of 4 correct.
```

Code Explanation:

Sample Emails: A list of emails is created, each with a subject, content, and a label indicating whether it is a phishing attempt (True) or a legitimate email (False).

User Interaction: The function phishing_awareness_training() presents each email to the employee. The employee is asked to evaluate the email and decide whether it is a phishing attempt by typing "yes" or "no."

Feedback Mechanism: After each decision, the program provides immediate feedback, explaining why the email was classified as phishing or legitimate. This helps reinforce learning.

Results: At the end of the simulation, the employee is provided with a score indicating how many emails they classified correctly out of the total number presented.

Benefits of the Example:

Interactive Training: The program is interactive, allowing employees to actively participate in learning to recognize phishing attempts.

Immediate Feedback: After each decision, employees receive feedback to understand why an email is phishing or legitimate, which helps reinforce their knowledge.

Easy Customization: The dataset of emails can be easily expanded or customized to suit different organizational contexts or common phishing scenarios.

This Python-based simulation could be a practical part of an organization's broader security awareness and training program, helping employees become more vigilant about identifying phishing attacks and other social engineering threats.

Chapter 10

Application Security

Learning Outcomes:

Upon completing this chapter, you will be able to:

- *Understand the importance of integrating security measures throughout the software development life cycle (SDLC).*
- *Identify common vulnerabilities and exposures (CVEs) in software applications and their impact.*
- *Explore methods for mitigating vulnerabilities through secure coding practices and comprehensive security testing.*
- *Implement DevSecOps principles to integrate security into continuous integration and deployment pipelines.*
- *Gain insights into the benefits of continuous monitoring and response for maintaining application security.*

10.1 Secure Software Development Life Cycle (SSDLC)

The Secure Software Development Life Cycle (SSDLC) is a methodology that incorporates security practices into each phase of the software development life cycle (SDLC) process. Rather than treating security as an afterthought, this approach ensures that applications are designed, developed, and deployed with security in mind from the very beginning. By embedding security at every stage, organizations can minimize vulnerabilities and prevent potential exploits before they reach production.

Key Phases:

Requirements Gathering: During this phase, security requirements should be identified alongside functional requirements. This includes identifying data security needs, compliance with regulatory standards, and potential risks that need to be mitigated.

Design: The architecture and design phase is critical for embedding security principles. This involves applying secure design patterns, performing threat modeling, and considering how security controls like authentication and encryption will be implemented.

Implementation: Secure coding practices must be followed to minimize common vulnerabilities. Developers should be trained in best practices, such as input validation, error handling, and avoiding hard-coded credentials.

Testing: Security testing should be an integral part of the testing phase. This includes both static (code analysis) and dynamic (runtime analysis) security testing to detect vulnerabilities. Testing environments should simulate real-world attack scenarios to identify weaknesses.

Deployment: Secure deployment processes involve configuring security settings, ensuring that applications are deployed in a hardened environment, and verifying that access controls are correctly implemented.

Maintenance: After deployment, the application must be continuously monitored for vulnerabilities, and updates or patches should be applied promptly. Ongoing maintenance also includes regularly auditing security controls to ensure compliance with evolving threats and regulations.

Benefits of SSDLC:

*Early Detection of Security Issues: I*dentifying vulnerabilities early in the development cycle is more cost-effective and efficient than addressing them post-deployment.

Reduced Costs: Fixing security issues during the design or coding phase is far less expensive than fixing them after a breach or production release.

Regulatory Compliance: Integrating security into the SDLC ensures that applications meet regulatory standards, such as GDPR, HIPAA, or PCI-DSS, which helps avoid fines or legal consequences.

Visual 10.1 illustrates key phases of secure software development lifecycle (SSDLC), where the security process is incorporated into the SDLC phases.

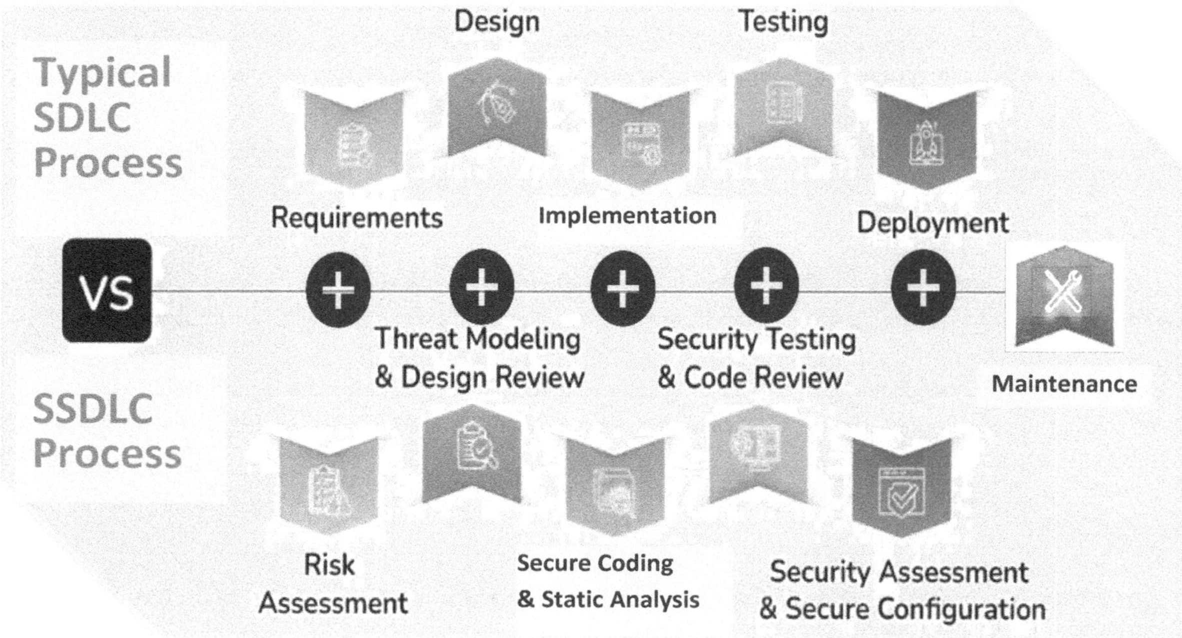

Visual 10.1: Key phases of the Secure Software Development Life Cycle (SSDLC).

10.2 Common Vulnerabilities and Exposures (CVEs)

Common Vulnerabilities and Exposures (CVEs) are publicly disclosed security vulnerabilities that affect software and hardware products. CVEs are assigned unique identifiers and published in a central repository, making it easier for organizations to track known vulnerabilities and apply patches to mitigate them.

Types of Vulnerabilities:

SQL Injection: A common attack that manipulates SQL queries to gain unauthorized access to databases. Attackers may retrieve, alter, or delete sensitive data by exploiting insecure input handling.

Cross-Site Scripting (XSS): This attack involves injecting malicious scripts into a web application to manipulate the behavior of web browsers. XSS allows attackers to steal user session data or redirect users to malicious websites.

Cross-Site Request Forgery (CSRF): In CSRF attacks, an attacker tricks a user into performing actions they did not intend, such as transferring funds or changing account details, by exploiting the user's authenticated session.

Buffer Overflow: This occurs when a program writes more data to a buffer than it can hold, causing the program to overwrite adjacent memory. Attackers can exploit buffer overflows to execute arbitrary code or crash the system.

Authentication Bypass: This vulnerability allows attackers to bypass authentication mechanisms and gain unauthorized access to sensitive information or system functionality.

CVE Mitigation Strategies:

Patch Management: Regularly apply patches and updates to address known vulnerabilities in software products. Having an automated patch management system ensures that critical vulnerabilities are addressed promptly.

Security Testing: Perform routine vulnerability assessments and penetration tests to detect and fix security issues before attackers can exploit them.

Secure Coding Practices: Follow best practices to prevent common vulnerabilities. Input validation, output encoding, and the principle of least privilege are essential practices to mitigate vulnerabilities.

Visual 10.2 illustrates some common application vulnerabilities and exposure (CVEs))highlighted in red), along with some mitigation strategies (highlighted in yellow).

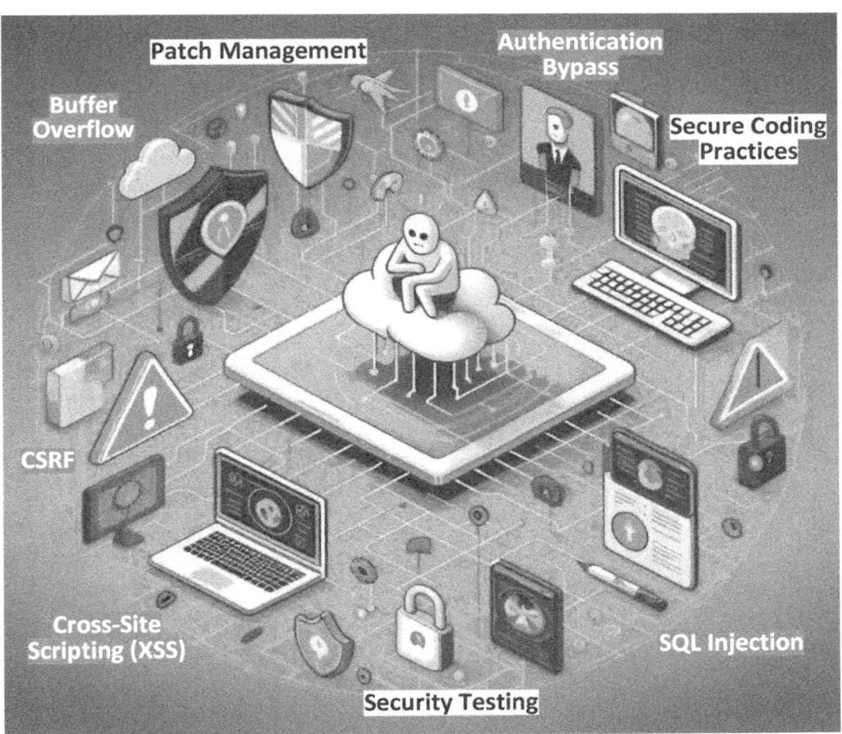

Visual 10.2: Common application vulnerabilities and exposure (CVEs) and mitigation strategies

10.3 Static and Dynamic Application Security Testing

Security testing is crucial in identifying vulnerabilities during and after the development phase. Two primary testing methodologies—Static Application Security Testing (SAST) and Dynamic Application Security Testing (DAST)—are used to ensure comprehensive security coverage.

Static Application Security Testing (SAST)*:* SAST is a white-box testing approach that analyzes the source code, bytecode, or binaries for security vulnerabilities without executing the program. SAST identifies vulnerabilities early in the development cycle and provides detailed insights into insecure code patterns.

Benefits: SAST tools, such as Fortify and Veracode, help detect vulnerabilities like hard-coded credentials, buffer overflows, and injection flaws during the coding phase.

Dynamic Application Security Testing (DAST): DAST is a black-box testing approach that simulates real-world attacks on running applications to identify security vulnerabilities at runtime. DAST helps discover issues such as configuration errors, authentication flaws, and insecure session management.

Benefits: DAST tools, including OWASP ZAP and Burp Suite, are used to test applications in their production-like environments. They help uncover vulnerabilities that may arise due to interaction with external systems or during user interactions.

By combining SAST and DAST, organizations can comprehensively identify security flaws in their code and production environments, ensuring more robust application security.

10.4 DevSecOps and Continuous Security Integration

DevSecOps is the practice of integrating security into DevOps processes, fostering collaboration between development, operations, and security teams to deliver secure software at speed.

Key DevSecOps Principles:
Shift-Left Security: This principle emphasizes embedding security earlier in the development cycle rather than waiting until the end. Security practices, such as code scanning and vulnerability assessments, should be performed continuously during development.

Automation: Automated security testing is essential to ensure that security checks, such as vulnerability scans and compliance checks, are part of the continuous integration/continuous deployment (CI/CD) pipeline.

Culture of Collaboration: DevSecOps encourages collaboration among developers, operations, and security teams, ensuring that security is a shared responsibility across the organization.

Continuous Security Integration:
Continuous security integration means incorporating security testing into the CI/CD pipeline. This ensures that security checks, such as SAST and DAST, are automatically triggered every time new code is pushed. Providing immediate feedback to developers on vulnerabilities allows for rapid remediation.

Automation in Security Testing: Tools such as Checkmarx (SAST) and OWASP ZAP (DAST) can be integrated into CI/CD pipelines to perform automated security checks, helping detect vulnerabilities during each development iteration.

Continuous Monitoring and Response: Post-deployment monitoring is critical to detect and respond to emerging threats. This includes monitoring application logs for suspicious behavior, detecting anomalies, and responding promptly to mitigate risks.

Visual 10.3 illustrates continuous security integration techniques.

Visual 10.3: Continuous security integration techniques.

10.5 Summary

In this chapter, we explored the Secure Software Development Life Cycle (SDLC), emphasizing the importance of integrating security throughout the development process. We discussed Common Vulnerabilities and Exposures (CVEs) and the importance of mitigation strategies like patch management and secure coding practices. Additionally, we reviewed the value of Static and Dynamic Application Security Testing (SAST and DAST) in identifying vulnerabilities early in development and during runtime. Finally, we explored the principles of DevSecOps and how continuous security integration enhances application security by automating security testing and monitoring.

Exercise 10

1. Scenario Analysis: Analyze a hypothetical application development scenario and identify potential security vulnerabilities at each phase of the SDLC.

2. Case Study Review: Review a case study of a recent CVE and propose mitigation strategies that could have prevented or minimized its impact.

3. Security Testing Practice: Conduct a hands-on session using a static or dynamic application security testing tool (e.g., Fortify, OWASP ZAP) to identify vulnerabilities in a sample application.

4. DevSecOps Implementation: Develop a plan to integrate security into a CI/CD pipeline using DevSecOps principles. Outline specific security checks and automation steps to be included.

Example Python Code for
Secure Coding for SQL injection

Context:

This example highlights the importance of secure coding practices in software development, particularly in defending against SQL injection attacks. By using parameterized queries, the code demonstrates how to safely handle user input when inserting data into a database. This approach prevents malicious SQL code from altering the database, a common vulnerability in unsecured applications.

Usefulness:

- Preventing SQL Injection: Mitigates SQL injection risks by properly handling user inputs.
- Data Integrity: Ensures that only valid data is inserted into the database, maintaining integrity.
- Secure Software Development: Encourages secure coding practices, reducing vulnerabilities in applications.

Input Features:

- Username: The user's chosen username, securely inserted into the database.
- Password: The user's password, securely handled to avoid exposure to SQL injection risks.
- Parameterized Query: A method used to safely insert user-provided data, preventing unauthorized database modifications.

Code:

```
import sqlite3

# Function to insert user input into a database securely
def insert_user(username, password):
    # Connect to SQLite database
    conn = sqlite3.connect('users.db')
    cursor = conn.cursor()

    # Use parameterized query to insert data safely
    insert_query = "INSERT INTO users (username, password) VALUES (?, ?)"
    cursor.execute(insert_query, (username, password))

    # Commit changes and close connection
    conn.commit()
    conn.close()

# Main program to demonstrate secure input handling
if __name__ == "__main__":
    # Get user input (normally from a web form or API call)
    username = input("Enter username: ")
    password = input("Enter password: ")

    # Call function to insert user data into database securely
    insert_user(username, password)

    print("User data inserted securely.")
```

Code Explanation:

SQLite Database Connection: The script connects to an SQLite database (users.db) where user data is stored.

Secure Input Handling: User inputs (username and password) are obtained using input() function. In real applications, these would come from user inputs via a web form or API.

Parameterized Query: To prevent SQL injection attacks, the script uses parameterized queries (cursor.execute()) instead of string concatenation. This method ensures that user inputs are treated as data and not executable SQL code.

Insertion Function: The insert_user() function handles the insertion of user data into the database. It takes username and password as parameters and securely inserts them using the parameterized query.

Commit and Close: After executing the query, changes are committed (conn.commit()) to the database, and the connection is closed (conn.close()).

Chapter 11

Cloud Security

Learning Outcomes:

Upon completing this chapter, you will be able to:

- *Understand the fundamental concepts and components of cloud security.*
- *Explore the Shared Responsibility Model and its implications for cloud security management.*
- *Identify security best practices specific to Infrastructure as a Service (IaaS), Platform as a Service (PaaS), and Software as a Service (SaaS) cloud models.*
- *Learn about data protection strategies, including encryption and data privacy in cloud environments.*
- *Gain insights into compliance requirements and legal considerations related to cloud security.*

11.1 Cloud Security Fundamentals

Cloud security refers to a set of policies, controls, technologies, and procedures designed to protect cloud-based systems, data, and infrastructure from cyber threats. Given the dynamic nature of cloud environments, organizations must ensure they address security concerns such as unauthorized access, data breaches, and regulatory compliance.

Key Considerations:

Multi-tenancy: Cloud environments often host multiple clients on shared infrastructure. Security measures must prevent one client from accessing or affecting another's data or resources.

Virtualization: Virtualization is at the core of cloud infrastructure. Security practices should ensure the isolation of virtual machines (VMs) and containers from one another to avoid cross-contamination of resources.

Network Security: Secure network configurations, including firewalls and intrusion detection systems (IDS), are essential to protect data transmitted across the internet and between cloud services.

Identity and Access Management (IAM): Controlling access to cloud resources through strong IAM policies is critical to ensuring only authorized users can access sensitive data or applications.

By incorporating these elements, organizations can create a secure cloud environment that protects sensitive information and mitigates risks.

11.2 Shared Responsibility Model

The Shared Responsibility Model outlines the division of security responsibilities between cloud service providers (CSPs) and cloud customers (organizations). While CSPs manage the security of the cloud infrastructure, customers must secure their data, applications, and user access within the cloud.

Key Responsibilities:

CSP Responsibilities:
Physical Security: Securing data centers, servers, and physical network infrastructure.

Platform Security: Maintaining and securing the underlying cloud platform, including hardware and software updates.

Compliance: Ensuring cloud infrastructure complies with global or regional regulations and certifications.

Customer Responsibilities:
Data Protection: Implementing encryption and access controls to secure data stored in the cloud.

Applications: Securing applications and ensuring they are free from vulnerabilities.

Identity Management: Managing user roles, permissions, and authentication to control access to resources.

The division of responsibilities varies based on the cloud model (IaaS, PaaS, or SaaS), which customers must understand to avoid security gaps.

11.3 Security Best Practices for IaaS, PaaS, and SaaS

Cloud environments present distinct challenges depending on the type of service provided. Therefore, security best practices must be adapted to match the unique requirements of each model: IaaS, PaaS, and SaaS.

IaaS (Infrastructure as a Service):
Virtual Networks: Segment virtual networks and apply firewall rules to isolate sensitive resources and minimize attack surfaces.

Identity and Access Management: Use multi-factor authentication (MFA) and least-privilege principles to limit access to critical resources.

Data Encryption: Encrypt sensitive data stored in virtual machines or databases, and ensure data is encrypted during transmission using strong encryption protocols.

PaaS (Platform as a Service):
Secure Development: Adopt secure coding practices, such as input validation and secure APIs, for applications built on PaaS platforms.

Automated Deployment: Automate application deployments with security checks integrated into continuous integration/continuous deployment (CI/CD) pipelines.

Monitoring and Logging: Implement security monitoring to track application performance and detect anomalies that could indicate security breaches.

SaaS (Software as a Service):
User Access Control: Manage user permissions to SaaS applications, ensuring that roles are appropriately defined and enforced.

Data Backup and Recovery: Implement regular backups of SaaS application data and test recovery procedures to ensure business continuity.

Vendor Security Assurance: Evaluate the security certifications and compliance of SaaS vendors before entrusting them with sensitive data.

These practices ensure a robust defense against cloud-specific threats and help safeguard critical assets.

Visual 11.1 illustrates best practices for IaaS, PaaS and SaaS.

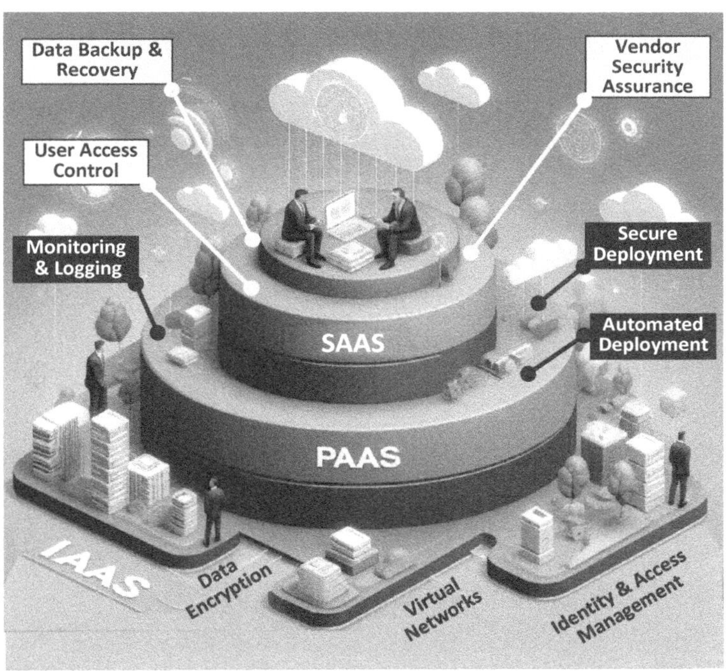

Visual 11.1: Best Practices for IaaS, PaaS and SaaS

11.4 Data Protection in the Cloud

Data protection is a central concern in cloud security, as organizations must ensure sensitive information remains secure at all times—whether it's in storage or being transmitted.

Data Encryption:
Encryption at Rest: Encrypting data stored in cloud databases or storage systems ensures that even if a breach occurs, the data remains unreadable without the decryption keys.

Encryption in Transit: Data should always be encrypted while in transit between clients and cloud services using secure transport protocols like SSL/TLS.

Data Privacy:
Data Masking: To protect sensitive data, masking techniques are applied to anonymize or pseudonymize personal information without affecting usability for processes like analytics or testing.

Compliance: Organizations using cloud services must comply with data protection laws such as GDPR and HIPAA, which impose strict requirements for how personal and sensitive data is stored, processed, and transferred.

By implementing encryption and privacy measures, organizations can maintain control over their data even in shared cloud environments.

11.5 Compliance and Legal Issues in Cloud Environments

Cloud environments are subject to various regulatory frameworks and legal challenges, particularly when data is stored across multiple regions or jurisdictions. Organizations must navigate these challenges to ensure compliance with applicable laws.

Regulatory Compliance:
GDPR: Organizations processing personal data of EU residents must comply with GDPR by implementing data protection measures, such as encryption and breach notification protocols.

HIPAA: Healthcare organizations using cloud-based systems must comply with HIPAA regulations to protect patient health information.

PCI DSS: E-commerce platforms using cloud services must adhere to the Payment Card Industry Data Security Standard (PCI DSS) to safeguard payment card data.

Legal Considerations:
Data Residency: Organizations must be aware of where their data is stored, as some countries impose strict data residency requirements that prevent the transfer of data outside national borders.

Contractual Agreements: Cloud service contracts should explicitly define security responsibilities, breach notification procedures, and compliance obligations to avoid ambiguity in the event of a breach or regulatory audit.

Incident Response: A clearly defined incident response plan for cloud environments is essential. It should outline roles, procedures, and timelines for responding to security incidents affecting cloud services.

Failure to comply with these regulations can result in significant legal and financial penalties.

11.6 Summary

This chapter explored the essential aspects of cloud security, from understanding the Shared Responsibility Model to applying best practices for securing IaaS, PaaS, and SaaS environments. We also discussed data protection strategies, such as encryption and privacy measures, and covered the regulatory and legal considerations that organizations must address when adopting cloud technologies. By implementing these strategies, organizations can better protect their data, ensure compliance, and manage the risks associated with cloud computing.

Exercise 11

1. Shared Responsibility Analysis: Evaluate a cloud service provider's Shared Responsibility Model and identify specific security responsibilities for both the provider and the customer.

2. IaaS Security Configuration: Develop a security configuration plan for an IaaS environment, including network segmentation and access control measures.

3. SaaS Vendor Assessment: Assess the security practices of a SaaS vendor using a checklist that includes data privacy, encryption, and compliance with industry standards.

4. Legal Compliance Scenario: Analyze a scenario involving cross-border data transfer in the cloud and identify potential legal and compliance challenges.

Example Python Code for Cloud Security (a)

Context:

This Python script demonstrates basic encryption and decryption of sensitive data, a common cloud security practice to protect data in transit or at rest. In cloud environments, data encryption is essential to safeguard information from unauthorized access, ensuring that sensitive data remains secure even if intercepted or improperly accessed.

Usefulness:

- Data Security: Encrypting data before storing it in the cloud helps protect it from unauthorized access.
- Confidentiality: Ensures that sensitive information remains confidential, a critical requirement in cloud storage.
- Compliance: Helps meet regulatory requirements (e.g., GDPR, HIPAA) for secure handling of sensitive data in cloud services.

Input Features:

- Encryption Key: A cryptographic key used to encrypt and decrypt data, simulating secure key management practices in cloud services.
- Sensitive Data: The actual data to be encrypted, representing confidential information stored or transferred in the cloud.
- Cipher Suite: A secure method (Fernet in this example) for encrypting and decrypting data to prevent unauthorized access.

Code:

```
from cryptography.fernet import Fernet

# Generate a key for encryption and decryption (this should be securely stored in a real
scenario)
def generate_key():
    return Fernet.generate_key()

# Encrypt data using a generated key
def encrypt_data(key, data):
    cipher_suite = Fernet(key)
    encrypted_data = cipher_suite.encrypt(data.encode())
    return encrypted_data

# Decrypt data using the same key
def decrypt_data(key, encrypted_data):
    cipher_suite = Fernet(key)
    decrypted_data = cipher_suite.decrypt(encrypted_data).decode()
    return decrypted_data

# Example usage
if __name__ == "__main__":
    # Generate a key
    key = generate_key()

    # Data to be encrypted
    sensitive_data = "This is sensitive information."
```

```
    # Encrypt data
    encrypted_data = encrypt_data(key, sensitive_data)
    print(f"Encrypted data: {encrypted_data}")

    # Decrypt data
    decrypted_data = decrypt_data(key, encrypted_data)
    print(f"Decrypted data: {decrypted_data}")
```

Output:

```
Encrypted data: b'gAAAAABmldldno17kd5pw-
TmBxDZBPbk4GSLR4h4Fm20zLuu8zrFHkt7pRchvfkuiI5whCiQrvWRVlsRsYJu9rmOE3129ied1XIIdZIoic5JpFp9xEF
cCsw='
Decrypted data: This is sensitive information.
```

Code Explanation:

Key Generation: The generate_key() function generates a symmetric encryption key using Fernet from the cryptography library.

Encryption: The encrypt_data() function takes the encryption key and sensitive data (sensitive_data in this example) as inputs, encrypts the data, and returns the encrypted bytes.

Decryption: The decrypt_data() function uses the same encryption key to decrypt the encrypted data and returns the original plaintext.

Example Usage: In the if __name__ == "__main__": block, a key is generated, and a sample sensitive string (sensitive_data) is encrypted and decrypted. This simulates the process of securing data using encryption, a crucial aspect of cloud security to protect data at rest.

Simulation of Cloud Security:
To simulate broader aspects of cloud security, consider extending this example to include scenarios like:

- *Access Control:* Implement role-based access control (RBAC) to simulate managing permissions and access levels.

- *Logging and Monitoring:* Integrate logging mechanisms to track and monitor access and activities within the simulated environment.

- *Network Security:* Simulate secure network configurations, such as virtual private clouds (VPCs), subnets, and security groups.

- *Compliance and Governance:* Implement checks to simulate compliance with regulations and governance frameworks, such as GDPR or HIPAA.

By combining these simulated scenarios with appropriate Python libraries and frameworks, we can gain a practical understanding of cloud security principles and practices.

Example Python Code for Cloud Security (b)

Context:

This Python code demonstrates basic Access Control in AWS by using IAM (Identity and Access Management) to securely manage permissions and roles. In cloud environments like AWS, setting up precise access control policies is essential for limiting user and service permissions, thus enhancing security by following the principle of least privilege.

Usefulness:

- Access Control: IAM roles and policies enable administrators to restrict access to specific cloud resources, reducing the risk of unauthorized access.
- Resource Isolation: IAM provides granular control over which resources (like EC2 instances) can interact with other services (e.g., S3), enhancing cloud security.
- Compliance: Access management supports regulatory compliance by ensuring only authorized users and services can access sensitive cloud data and operations.

Input Features:

- IAM Role: Defines a role (e.g., MyEC2Role) that specifies permissions for EC2 instances, allowing them to securely access other AWS services.
- Policy Attachment: Assigns a policy (AmazonS3ReadOnlyAccess) to the role, controlling which actions the instance can perform on other services.
- Instance Profile: Applies the IAM role to an EC2 instance, enabling the instance to interact with AWS resources securely.

Code:

```
import boto3

# Create IAM client
iam = boto3.client('iam')

# Create a new IAM role
response = iam.create_role(
    RoleName='MyEC2Role',
    AssumeRolePolicyDocument='''{
        "Version": "2012-10-17",
        "Statement": [
            {
              "Effect": "Allow",
              "Principal": {
                "Service": "ec2.amazonaws.com"
              },
              "Action": "sts:AssumeRole"
            }
        ]
    }'''
)

# Attach an IAM policy to the role
response = iam.attach_role_policy(
    RoleName='MyEC2Role',
    PolicyArn='arn:aws:iam::aws:policy/AmazonS3ReadOnlyAccess'
)
```

```
# Create a new EC2 instance with the IAM role
ec2 = boto3.resource('ec2')
instance = ec2.create_instances(
    ImageId='ami-12345678',
    MinCount=1,
    MaxCount=1,
    InstanceType='t2.micro',
    IamInstanceProfile={
        'Arn': 'arn:aws:iam::123456789012:instance-profile/MyEC2Role'
    }
)

print("EC2 instance created with IAM role 'MyEC2Role'.")
```

Code Explanation:

Context: In cloud environments like AWS, IAM (Identity and Access Management) plays a crucial role in ensuring that only authorized entities (users, applications, or services) have access to specific resources.

Code Explanation:

- IAM Role Creation: Defines a new IAM role named MyEC2Role that allows EC2 instances to assume this role (sts:AssumeRole).
- Policy Attachment: Attaches the AmazonS3ReadOnlyAccess policy to MyEC2Role, granting read-only access to S3 buckets.
- EC2 Instance Creation: Creates a new EC2 instance (t2.micro) and assigns it the MyEC2Role IAM role for access permissions.

Importance:
Cloud security measures such as IAM ensure that access to cloud resources is controlled and monitored, reducing the risk of unauthorized access and data breaches. Implementing robust access control mechanisms like IAM policies is essential for maintaining a secure cloud infrastructure.

This example illustrates a fundamental aspect of cloud security, focusing on IAM roles and policies to control access permissions within AWS, contributing to a comprehensive cybersecurity strategy in cloud computing environments.

Chapter 12

Mobile and IoT Security

Learning Outcomes:

Upon completing this chapter, you will be able to:

- *Understand the security challenges and threats specific to mobile devices and IoT ecosystems.*
- *Explore security measures and best practices for securing mobile devices against malware, phishing, and data leakage.*
- *Identify key security risks associated with IoT devices, including lack of standardization and firmware vulnerabilities.*
- *Learn about best practices for securing mobile and IoT devices, including authentication, data encryption, and firmware updates.*

12.1 Mobile Device Security

As mobile devices continue to serve as essential tools for communication, business, and personal activities, they face unique security challenges. Mobile device security encompasses policies, technologies, and procedures to protect against unauthorized access, data breaches, and malicious attacks.

Mobile Threat Landscape:

Malware: Malicious software specifically targeting mobile devices to steal sensitive information, monitor activities, or disrupt device operations. Mobile malware variants include Trojans, spyware, and ransomware.

Phishing: Cybercriminals often employ deceptive messages, fake websites, and malicious apps to trick users into revealing credentials or installing malware.

Data Leakage: Unintentional or unauthorized sharing of sensitive information stored on or transmitted from mobile devices due to poorly configured apps or insecure communication channels.

Unauthorized Access: Weak authentication measures or physical theft of devices can lead to security breaches and data theft.

Security Measures:

Device Encryption: Encrypt all data stored on mobile devices to prevent unauthorized access, even if the device is lost or stolen.

Mobile Device Management (MDM): Implement MDM solutions to enforce security policies, monitor device usage, and remotely wipe data from compromised devices.

App Permissions: Regularly review and control permissions granted to apps to limit their access to sensitive data such as location, contacts, and stored files.

Security Updates: Keep devices up to date with the latest security patches to mitigate known vulnerabilities and exploits.

12.2 IoT Device Security Challenges

The rapid proliferation of IoT devices introduces new security risks to networks and data. IoT devices often operate with minimal oversight, lack standard security protocols, and may not receive regular updates, making them vulnerable targets.

IoT Security Risks:

Lack of Standardization: IoT devices vary in terms of security capabilities and standards, creating inconsistencies and gaps in security across connected environments.

Weak Authentication: Many IoT devices come with default credentials or weak authentication mechanisms, increasing the risk of unauthorized access.

Data Privacy: IoT devices collect vast amounts of data, raising concerns about potential exposure of sensitive information if devices are compromised.

Firmware Vulnerabilities: Outdated or insecure firmware can be exploited by attackers to gain control over IoT devices or disrupt services.

Security Considerations:

Network Segmentation: Isolate IoT devices from critical systems by creating dedicated, segmented networks to minimize the impact of breaches.

Authentication and Access Control: Implement robust authentication mechanisms, such as multi-factor authentication (MFA), for accessing IoT devices and services.

Data Encryption: Encrypt data transmitted between IoT devices and cloud services to safeguard information from interception or tampering.

Regular Audits: Conduct security audits and vulnerability assessments of IoT devices and their networks to identify and address potential risks.

Visual 12.1 illustrates mobile and IOT security risks as well as the considerations to mitigate them.

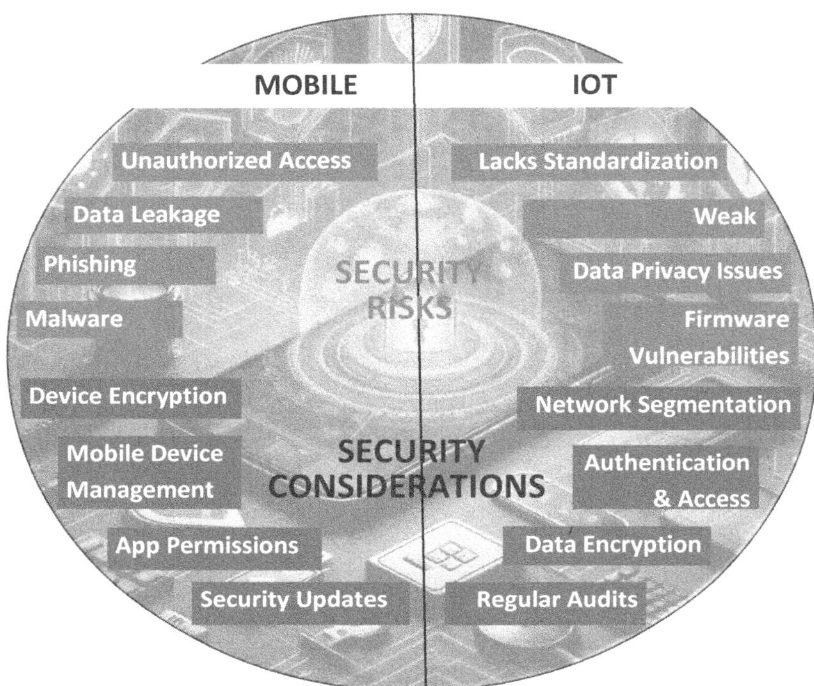

Visual 12.1: Mobile and IOT security risks and considerations

12.3 Best Practices for Securing Mobile and IoT Devices

Mobile Devices:

Strong Authentication: Use biometric authentication methods (e.g., fingerprint recognition or facial recognition) in addition to traditional passwords for enhanced security.

Data Backup: Regularly back up data stored on mobile devices to prevent data loss in case of device failure or breach.

Secure Wi-Fi: Avoid connecting to unsecured public Wi-Fi networks, and use virtual private networks (VPNs) to ensure secure communication over the internet.

IoT Devices:

Change Default Credentials: Replace default passwords on IoT devices with strong, unique passwords immediately upon deployment.

Update Firmware: Regularly update device firmware to patch known vulnerabilities and strengthen device security.

Monitor Device Behavior: Implement monitoring solutions to detect abnormal activities in IoT devices, which could indicate security breaches or attacks.

Physical Security: Ensure physical access to IoT devices is restricted to authorized personnel only, reducing the risk of tampering or unauthorized modifications.

12.4 Case Studies on Mobile and IoT Security Incidents

Examples of Security Incidents:

Mobile Device Malware: High-profile instances of mobile malware infections have resulted in the theft of banking credentials, financial losses, and unauthorized surveillance of users.

IoT Botnets: Compromised IoT devices, such as routers and security cameras, have been used in large-scale distributed denial-of-service (DDoS) attacks that disrupt services and networks.

Privacy Breaches: Poorly secured IoT devices have led to data leaks exposing personal information, including home surveillance footage and health data.

Lessons Learned:

Importance of Security Awareness: Educating users about security risks and best practices is essential for preventing incidents and mitigating their impact.

Need for Security by Design: Security should be integrated into the design and development of mobile and IoT devices, emphasizing robust authentication, secure firmware, and data protection.

Collaboration: Manufacturers, developers, and security researchers must collaborate to identify and address vulnerabilities proactively and improve overall device security.

12.5 Summary

This chapter explored the unique security challenges associated with mobile and IoT devices, including the threat landscape, security measures, and specific challenges related to IoT. By implementing security best practices such as strong authentication, encryption, network segmentation, and regular updates, organizations can enhance the security of their mobile and IoT ecosystems. Additionally, understanding case studies of past incidents and the lessons learned reinforces the importance of a proactive, collaborative approach to mobile and IoT security.

Exercise 12

1. Mobile Device Security Audit: Conduct a security audit of mobile devices within your organization, identifying potential vulnerabilities and recommending mitigation strategies.

2. IoT Device Vulnerability Assessment: Assess the security posture of IoT devices deployed in a simulated environment, identifying firmware vulnerabilities and proposing remediation steps.

3. Case Study Analysis: Analyze a recent security incident involving either mobile devices or IoT devices, outlining key factors contributing to the incident and proposing preventive measures.

Example Python Code for Mobile Application Threat Detection

Context:

Mobile security threats are prevalent due to the widespread use of smartphones for sensitive activities, including banking, messaging, and personal data management. This example demonstrates how a malicious app might request excessive permissions and exfiltrate data. It underscores the importance of following security best practices, such as using official app stores, reviewing permissions, and keeping security software up-to-date, to mitigate the risk of data theft.

Scenario:

- Download and Installation: A user downloads a game app from an unofficial source, which is not verified by Google Play Store or Apple App Store.
- Malicious Activity: The app requests unnecessary permissions, such as access to contacts or SMS, which are irrelevant to a game.
- Data Theft: Once installed, the app covertly collects sensitive information and sends it to a remote server controlled by an attacker.

Mitigation Strategies:

- Use Official App Stores: Only download apps from trusted sources.
- Review App Permissions: Be cautious of apps requesting permissions unrelated to their function.
- Install Security Software: Use mobile security apps that scan for malware.
- Keep Software Updated: Regularly update the operating system and apps.
- Exercise Link Caution: Avoid clicking on links from untrusted sources to prevent potential malware downloads.

The Python code below simulates a script mimicking the behavior of a malicious mobile app requesting excessive permissions and exfiltrating data. This serves as a reminder of potential mobile security risks and the need for vigilance.

Code:

```
import time

class MaliciousApp:
    def __init__(self, app_name):
        self.app_name = app_name
        self.permissions = []

    def request_permissions(self, *permissions):
        self.permissions.extend(permissions)

    def steal_data(self):
        if 'contacts' in self.permissions:
            print("Stealing contacts...")
            # Simulate stealing contacts (not implemented for real, just an example)
            time.sleep(2)
            print("Contacts stolen.")
        if 'location' in self.permissions:
            print("Accessing user's location...")
            # Simulate accessing location (not implemented for real, just an example)
            time.sleep(1)
            print("Location data accessed.")
```

```
def main():
    app_name = "GameApp"
    malicious_app = MaliciousApp(app_name)

    # Simulate requesting permissions
    malicious_app.request_permissions('contacts', 'location', 'camera')

    # Simulate stealing data based on permissions
    malicious_app.steal_data()

if __name__ == "__main__":
    main()
```

Output:

```
Stealing contacts...
Contacts stolen.
Accessing user's location...
Location data accessed.
```

Code Explanation:

MaliciousApp Class: Represents a simple simulation of a mobile app. It has methods to request permissions (request_permissions) and to simulate data theft (steal_data).

Permissions: In the example, the app requests permissions for accessing contacts, location, and camera. These are typical permissions that a malicious app might request to collect sensitive user information.

Stealing Data: The steal_data method simulates accessing and exfiltrating sensitive data. For example, it prints messages indicating the simulated process of stealing contacts and accessing location data.

Chapter 13

Advanced Persistent Threats

Learning Outcomes:

Upon completing this chapter, you will be able to:

- *Define Advanced Persistent Threats (APTs) and recognize their characteristics and objectives.*
- *Identify common techniques and tactics used by APTs to gain unauthorized access and achieve their goals.*
- *Understand detection techniques such as behavioral analysis and endpoint detection, along with mitigation strategies to counter APTs.*
- *Analyze case studies of notable APT attacks to understand their impact and the lessons learned.*
- *Develop proactive measures and incident response plans to defend against APTs effectively.*

13.1 Understanding APTs

Advanced Persistent Threats (APTs) represent a highly sophisticated form of cyberattack, typically orchestrated by well-funded and skilled adversaries. These attackers—often state-sponsored or financially motivated—aim to infiltrate organizations and maintain undetected access over an extended period. Their objectives range from espionage and intellectual property theft to sabotage and financial gain.

Characteristics:

Stealth: APTs aim to remain undetected for prolonged periods, using advanced evasion techniques to bypass security measures.

Persistence: Attackers maintain a continuous presence on compromised systems, ensuring they can access and extract valuable data over time.

Advanced Techniques: APTs leverage a variety of tactics, from exploiting zero-day vulnerabilities to launching highly targeted phishing campaigns.

13.2 Techniques and Tactics Used by APTs

APTs employ a combination of sophisticated techniques and multi-stage attack strategies. The following tactics highlight common methods used by APT actors to compromise their targets:
Common Techniques:

Phishing and Spear Phishing: Customized emails that contain malicious links or attachments, tricking specific individuals into disclosing credentials or installing malware.

Watering Hole Attacks: Compromising websites known to be frequented by target organizations or individuals, then delivering malware to visitors.

Supply Chain Compromise: Gaining access to a target network by compromising third-party vendors, software providers, or suppliers.

Zero-Day Exploits: Exploiting vulnerabilities that are unknown to the software vendor and have no available patches, enabling attackers to infiltrate systems undetected.

Credential Theft: Stealing usernames, passwords, or other authentication information through keyloggers, social engineering, or phishing attacks.

Tactics:

Initial Compromise: The first point of entry, often achieved through phishing or exploiting a software vulnerability.

Lateral Movement: Once inside, attackers move across systems and networks to gain access to higher-value resources.

Data Exfiltration: Extracting sensitive data, such as intellectual property or financial information, without alerting security measures.

Persistence: Establishing backdoors, rootkits, or remote access tools to ensure long-term access to compromised systems.

Visual 13.1 illustrates how Advanced Persistent Threats works.

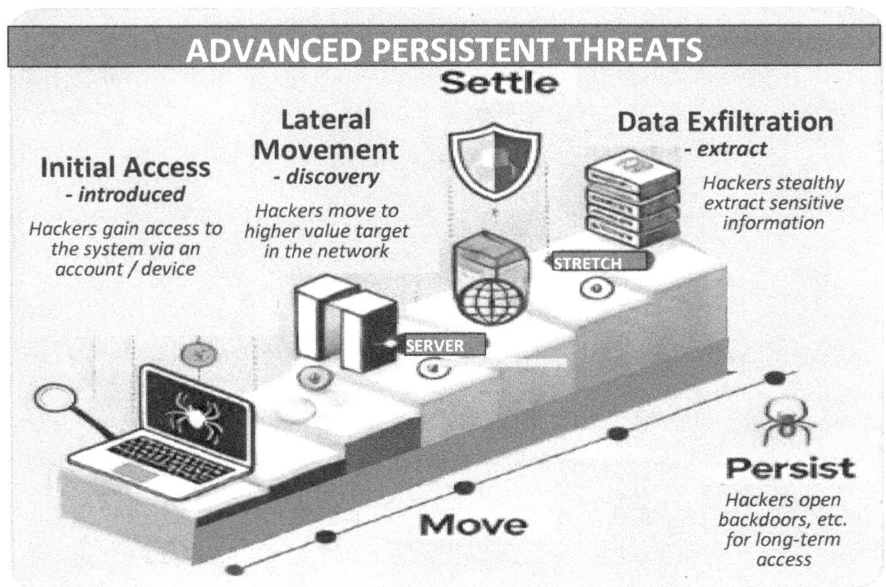

Visual 13.1: Tactic used in Advanced Persistent Threats (APT)

13.3 Detection and Mitigation Strategies

Detecting and mitigating APTs requires a comprehensive and proactive security strategy. Since APTs often evade traditional defenses, organizations need to implement advanced detection techniques and layered defenses.

Detection Techniques:

Behavioral Analysis: Monitoring for anomalous activities or deviations from normal behavior patterns, such as unusual login times or unexpected data transfers.

Threat Intelligence: Leveraging global threat intelligence feeds to identify indicators of compromise (IOCs) related to known APT actors or campaigns.

Endpoint Detection and Response (EDR): Using EDR tools to detect, investigate, and respond to malicious activities on endpoints.

Network Traffic Analysis: Analyzing network traffic for signs of data exfiltration, lateral movement, or command-and-control communications.

Mitigation Strategies:

Defense-in-Depth: Implementing multiple layers of security, including firewalls, intrusion detection systems (IDS), and multi-factor authentication, to create barriers at every potential entry point.

User Education: Training employees to recognize and avoid phishing attempts and encouraging secure behavior to reduce the likelihood of successful social engineering attacks.

Patch Management: Regularly updating systems with the latest security patches to close vulnerabilities before they can be exploited by APT actors.

Incident Response Planning: Developing a well-defined incident response plan that outlines steps for detecting, containing, and recovering from APT incidents.

13.4 Case Studies of APT Attacks

APTs have been responsible for some of the most high-profile and damaging cyberattacks in recent history. Examining case studies of these attacks can provide valuable insights into APT tactics and strategies:

Examples:

APT29 (Cozy Bear): Linked to the Russian government, APT29 is known for espionage activities targeting governments, research institutions, and private sector organizations. It gained widespread attention for its role in the 2016 U.S. election interference.

APT28 (Fancy Bear): Another Russian-linked group, APT28, has been involved in cyber operations against military and governmental organizations. The group was responsible for the NotPetya ransomware attack, which caused extensive financial damage globally.

APT1 (Comment Crew): Alleged to be backed by the Chinese government, APT1 has been involved in industrial espionage, targeting U.S. corporations to steal trade secrets and intellectual property.

Lessons Learned:

Importance of Attribution: While identifying the exact source of an APT attack can be challenging, understanding the threat actors' motivations and techniques can inform defensive measures.

Continuous Monitoring: APTs often remain undetected for extended periods, emphasizing the need for continuous monitoring and anomaly detection.

Collaboration: Sharing threat intelligence and collaborating with industry peers and law enforcement agencies can help organizations identify threats earlier and respond more effectively.

13.5 Summary

This chapter provided an in-depth exploration of Advanced Persistent Threats (APTs), their characteristics, and the tactics they employ to compromise and persist in systems. By examining detection techniques such as behavioral analysis and EDR, along with real-world case studies, organizations can develop more robust defense strategies. Proactive measures, including incident response planning, patch management, and user education, are essential in mitigating the long-term risks posed by APTs.

Exercise 13

1. Tabletop Exercise: Conduct a simulated APT attack on your organization's network, walking through the critical response actions, detection methods, and communication strategies necessary to mitigate the threat.

2. EDR Capabilities Evaluation: Assess the effectiveness of your organization's endpoint detection and response (EDR) tools in identifying and responding to APT activities. Provide recommendations for improvement.

3. APT Research: Research and analyze a recent APT attack that was not covered in the chapter. Identify the key tactics used and assess the impact on the affected organizations.

4. Incident Response Playbook: Develop an incident response playbook designed specifically for mitigating an APT attack. Include steps for containment, eradication, and recovery, as well as post-incident analysis.

Example Python Code for Advanced Persistent Threats (APTs) Detection

Context:
This Python example demonstrates an Advanced Persistent Threat (APT) detection system, which monitors network traffic and uses a simple anomaly detection model to identify suspicious activities. By comparing current traffic patterns against historical baselines, the system flags deviations that may indicate an ongoing APT attack. This proactive approach helps organizations detect potential threats early, reducing the likelihood of undetected data breaches or prolonged unauthorized access.

Usefulness:
- Early Threat Detection: Identifies unusual patterns that may signal an APT, allowing rapid response before the threat escalates.
- Enhanced Security Monitoring: Automates the detection of subtle, persistent attack patterns that are often missed by traditional security solutions.
- Reduced Manual Inspection: Supports cybersecurity teams by automating anomaly detection, helping to prioritize high-risk events for further investigation.

Input Features:
- Normal Traffic Data: Historical data representing standard network activity (e.g., packet count, login frequency, data transfer volume).
- Anomalous Traffic Data: Data that exhibits abnormal activity patterns linked to APTs, like high packet volumes, multiple failed login attempts, or large outbound data transfers.
- Detection Threshold: A threshold that differentiates between normal and suspicious behavior, optimizing detection accuracy and minimizing false positives.

Code:

```
import numpy as np
import matplotlib.pyplot as plt
from sklearn.ensemble import IsolationForest

# Simulated network traffic data (features: packet_count, login_attempts, data_transfer)
normal_traffic = np.array([
    [100, 5, 200],  # Normal traffic: packet count, login attempts, data transfer (in MB)
    [150, 3, 220],
    [120, 4, 210],
    [110, 6, 205],
    [130, 4, 215]
])

# Simulated anomalous traffic (APT-like behavior)
anomalous_traffic = np.array([
    [300, 20, 500],  # Unusually high packet count, frequent login attempts, large data transfer
(suspicious)
    [200, 2, 600],   # Large data transfer
    [50, 10, 1000],  # Abnormally low packet count, high data exfiltration
])

# Combine normal and anomalous traffic for testing
traffic_data = np.vstack([normal_traffic, anomalous_traffic])
```

```
# Isolation Forest for anomaly detection
model = IsolationForest(contamination=0.3)  # 30% contamination (expected anomalous data)
model.fit(normal_traffic)  # Train on normal traffic

# Predict anomalies (1: normal, -1: anomaly)
predictions = model.predict(traffic_data)

# Output the results
for i, pred in enumerate(predictions):
    if pred == -1:
        print(f"Traffic {i + 1}: Suspicious activity detected! (Potential APT)")
    else:
        print(f"Traffic {i + 1}: Normal activity.")

# Visualizing the traffic
plt.scatter(range(len(traffic_data)), traffic_data[:, 0], c=predictions, cmap='coolwarm')
plt.title('APT Detection: Packet Count Analysis')
plt.xlabel('Traffic Instance')
plt.ylabel('Packet Count')
plt.show()
---------------------------------------------------------------------------------
```

Sample run:

```
Traffic 1: Normal activity.
Traffic 2: Normal activity.
Traffic 3: Normal activity.
Traffic 4: Normal activity.
Traffic 5: Normal activity.
Traffic 6: Suspicious activity detected! (Potential APT)
Traffic 7: Suspicious activity detected! (Potential APT)
Traffic 8: Suspicious activity detected! (Potential APT)
```

Code Explanation:

Simulated Data: We create synthetic traffic data with three features for each instance:

- Packet Count: Number of network packets sent.
- Login Attempts: Number of login attempts in a session.
- Data Transfer: Amount of data transferred (in MB).

Normal Traffic: This dataset represents typical network behavior (e.g., moderate packet counts, login attempts, and data transfer).

Anomalous Traffic: This dataset simulates APT-like behavior, such as high packet counts (possible lateral movement), frequent login attempts (e.g., brute-force attack), and large outbound data transfers (e.g., data exfiltration).

Isolation Forest Model: The Isolation Forest algorithm is used for anomaly detection. It trains on normal traffic data and flags deviations as potential APT behaviors.

Detection and Output: The model predicts each traffic instance as either normal or suspicious (APT-like behavior). Suspicious activities are flagged as potential APTs.

Visualization: A simple scatter plot visualizes the packet count for each traffic instance, with normal traffic in one color and suspicious traffic in another.

Results:
Normal Traffic: The majority of traffic instances are classified as normal by the model.
Suspicious Traffic: The last three instances of the dataset, which exhibit APT-like behavior, are flagged as suspicious.

Benefits:
Behavioral Analysis: The code simulates how an organization can leverage machine learning to detect anomalous behaviors indicative of APTs in real-time.

Incident Response: Once suspicious activities are detected, the system can trigger incident response measures to contain and investigate the threats.

Scalability: This system can be easily scaled by integrating real network logs from SIEM tools and used as part of a broader threat detection and response framework.

Chapter 14

Blockchain and Its Impact on Cybersecurity

Learning Outcomes:

Upon completing this chapter, you will be able to:

- *Define blockchain technology and explain its key components, including decentralization, immutability, and cryptographic security.*
- *Describe the role of blockchain in enhancing cybersecurity by providing secure, transparent, and tamper-resistant solutions.*
- *Identify the various applications of blockchain in cybersecurity, such as decentralized identity management, secure data sharing, and IoT security.*
- *Explain how blockchain can improve data integrity and ensure secure financial transactions and communications.*
- *Compare different blockchain consensus mechanisms (e.g., Proof of Work, Proof of Stake, DPoS) and understand their advantages and limitations in terms of security and efficiency.*
- *Examine real-world case studies demonstrating the use of blockchain in enhancing cybersecurity.*
- *Evaluate the challenges and limitations of blockchain in cybersecurity, including scalability, energy consumption, and regulatory issues.*
- *Explore future trends in blockchain technology, including zero-knowledge proofs, cross-chain interoperability, and blockchain's role in securing emerging technologies like IoT and AI.*

14.1 Introduction to Blockchain Technology

Blockchain is a decentralized, distributed ledger technology designed to maintain a secure, immutable record of transactions across a network of nodes. Initially created to support Bitcoin, blockchain technology has since evolved, finding applications in various industries, particularly in enhancing cybersecurity. Its key components—decentralization, immutability, transparency, and cryptographic security—make it a powerful tool for ensuring data integrity, reducing fraud, and mitigating cyberattacks.

Key Features of Blockchain:

Decentralization: Blockchain removes the need for a centralized authority by distributing data across multiple nodes. This minimizes the risk of single points of failure, making the network more resilient to attacks.

Immutability: Once data is recorded in a blockchain, it cannot be altered without changing all subsequent blocks, making it nearly impossible to tamper with the data.

Transparency: All participants in the network have access to the same version of the ledger, ensuring that transactions are transparent and verifiable.

Cryptographic Security: Blockchain relies on cryptographic techniques like hashing to secure data and transactions, ensuring authenticity and preventing unauthorized alterations.

Blockchain's potential to revolutionize cybersecurity lies in its ability to offer secure, decentralized solutions to many existing security challenges, such as data breaches, fraud, and identity theft.

14.2 Blockchain in Cybersecurity

Blockchain can enhance cybersecurity through various mechanisms that ensure data integrity, secure identity management, and safe data sharing.

Enhancing Data Integrity
Blockchain guarantees data integrity by creating an immutable ledger where all transactions are cryptographically recorded. Any attempt to alter data would require changing every subsequent block, which is computationally infeasible, ensuring the authenticity and integrity of the data.

Decentralized Identity Management
Blockchain provides a decentralized approach to identity management, reducing reliance on centralized databases vulnerable to breaches. Self-sovereign identity (SSI) enables individuals to control their digital identities, which are verified and secured using blockchain, reducing the risks of identity theft and unauthorized access.

Secure Data Sharing
Blockchain allows secure data sharing between parties without requiring a trusted third party. In industries like healthcare, where sensitive data must be shared between organizations, blockchain ensures that all shared data is traceable and secure.

Smart Contracts: Self-executing contracts embedded in blockchain that automatically enforce terms and conditions, improving trust and reducing fraud in digital transactions.

Visual 14.1 illustrates the blockchain process (in black) and the validation process for a valid user (in green) and malicious user (in red).

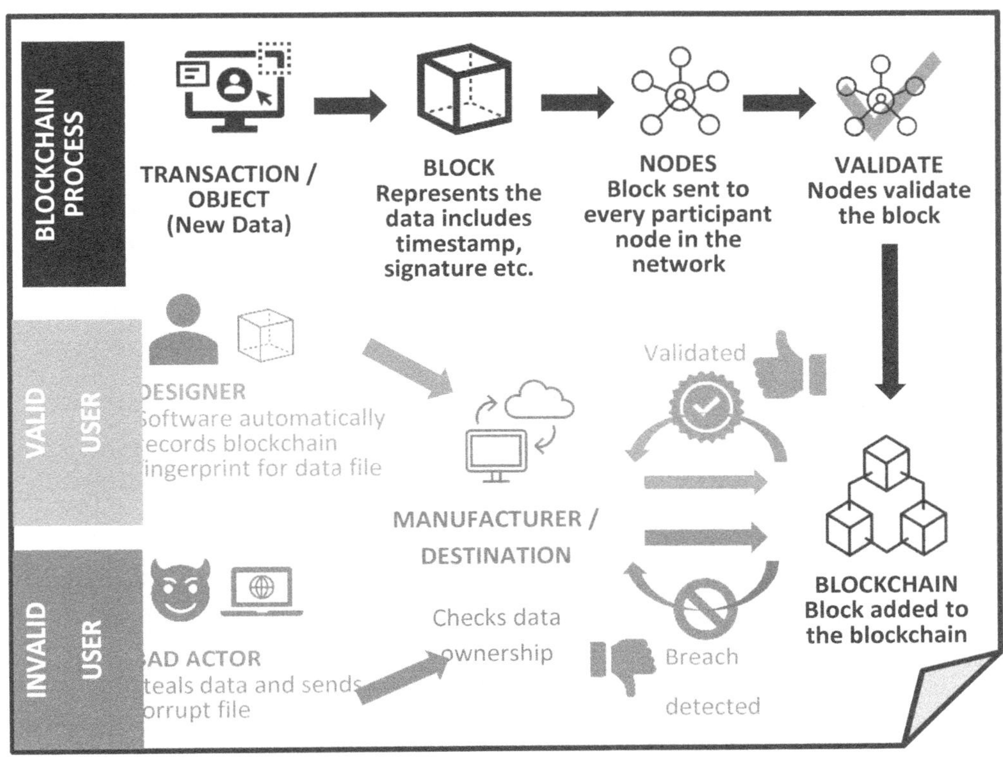

Visual 14.1: Blockchain process

14.3 Blockchain for Secure Transactions and Communication

Financial Transactions

Blockchain's use in cryptocurrency has shown its potential to secure financial transactions. By eliminating intermediaries and relying on decentralized networks, blockchain ensures that transactions are secure, transparent, and irreversible, which reduces fraud and enhances trust.

Blockchain in Secure Communications

Blockchain can be applied to secure communication channels, ensuring data integrity and confidentiality. Blockchain-based messaging platforms like Telegram and Signal leverage its cryptographic security to prevent unauthorized access to messages, creating immutable records of communication.

14.4 Blockchain-Based Cybersecurity Solutions

Blockchain for IoT Security
IoT devices are often vulnerable to cyberattacks due to weak security protocols. Blockchain can address these vulnerabilities by providing decentralized authentication and ensuring that only authorized devices communicate within a network, thereby protecting the integrity of IoT data.

Supply Chain Security
Blockchain provides transparency and traceability in supply chain management, ensuring that all transactions and movements of goods are securely recorded. This can help prevent fraud, counterfeiting, and tampering in industries such as pharmaceuticals, where security is paramount.

14.5 Consensus Mechanisms in Blockchain

Consensus mechanisms are critical to maintaining the security and integrity of blockchain networks. Different consensus algorithms ensure that nodes in the network agree on the validity of transactions.

Proof of Work (PoW)
Proof of Work (PoW) requires miners to solve complex cryptographic puzzles to validate transactions and add blocks to the blockchain. While secure, PoW is energy-intensive and slower compared to other methods.

Proof of Stake (PoS)
Proof of Stake (PoS) selects validators based on the number of tokens they hold and are willing to stake. PoS consumes far less energy than PoW and promotes long-term investment in the network by validators.

Delegated Proof of Stake (DPoS)
In DPoS, token holders vote for delegates who validate transactions on their behalf. DPoS increases scalability and is more efficient than PoW and PoS, making it suitable for large-scale applications.

14.6 Case Studies: Blockchain in Cybersecurity

Guardtime - Blockchain for Data Integrity
Guardtime's Keyless Signature Infrastructure (KSI) uses blockchain to secure the integrity of digital records for government and enterprise clients. KSI ensures that records are tamper-proof, protecting them from unauthorized alterations.

Estonia's National Blockchain Initiative
Estonia uses blockchain to secure a range of public services, from voting to healthcare records. This ensures that citizens' data is protected from tampering while maintaining transparency in government operations.

14.7 Challenges and Limitations of Blockchain in Cybersecurity

Despite its advantages, blockchain faces several challenges:

Scalability: As blockchain networks grow, they can struggle with scalability, leading to slower transaction processing times.

Energy Consumption: Consensus mechanisms like PoW require significant computational power, raising environmental concerns.

Regulatory Issues: The decentralized nature of blockchain can pose regulatory challenges, particularly in financial and healthcare industries where strict oversight is required.

14.8 Future of Blockchain in Cybersecurity

As blockchain technology evolves, it is expected to address some of its current limitations and find broader applications in cybersecurity. Emerging trends include:

Zero-Knowledge Proofs: Allowing one party to prove the validity of information without revealing the information itself.

Cross-Chain Interoperability: Enabling different blockchain networks to communicate and share data securely.

Blockchain in IoT and AI Security: Blockchain will play an increasing role in securing IoT and AI systems, ensuring data integrity, and enhancing trust between interconnected devices.

14.9 Summary

Blockchain offers significant potential to enhance cybersecurity by providing decentralized, transparent, and tamper-resistant solutions for securing data, identities, and communications. However, its adoption faces challenges related to scalability, energy consumption, and regulatory compliance. As blockchain continues to evolve, its applications in cybersecurity are expected to grow, particularly in areas such as IoT, data integrity, and decentralized identity management.

Exercise 14

1. Define blockchain and compare it with centralized systems: Discuss the benefits and challenges of blockchain for cybersecurity.

2. Explain blockchain's security features: Explore how immutability, cryptographic security, and consensus mechanisms enhance security.

3. Discuss decentralized identity management: How can blockchain address challenges in traditional identity management systems?

4. Evaluate consensus mechanisms: Compare Proof of Work, Proof of Stake, and Delegated Proof of Stake in terms of security and efficiency.

5. Case Study Analysis: Examine how blockchain is used to secure financial transactions or supply chains, and discuss the security advantages.

6. Blockchain for IoT Security: Discuss how blockchain can enhance security in IoT devices and ecosystems.

7. Challenges of Blockchain: Evaluate the limitations of blockchain, focusing on scalability and energy consumption, and propose solutions.

Example Python Code for Simulating a Simple Blockchain

Context:

The following Python code simulates a basic blockchain. Each block contains a list of transactions, a timestamp, a cryptographic hash of the previous block, and its own hash. This system ensures that once data is added to the blockchain, it cannot be altered without changing all subsequent blocks, providing data integrity and security.

Key Concepts Demonstrated:

- *Decentralization:* In this example, the blockchain is decentralized, meaning no central authority controls the system.
- *Immutability:* Once a block is added, its cryptographic hash links it to the previous block, preventing tampering.
- *Cryptographic Security:* SHA-256 hashing ensures that data within blocks is securely hashed and difficult to manipulate.

Input Features:

- Transactions: Simulated transactions between users, which will be stored in each block.
- Block Hashes: Cryptographic hashes that link blocks to one another, forming a chain.
- Timestamp: Records when each block is added to the blockchain.

Code:

```
import hashlib
import time

# Block class to define a single block in the blockchain
class Block:
    def __init__(self, previous_hash, transactions, timestamp=None):
        self.previous_hash = previous_hash
        self.transactions = transactions
        self.timestamp = timestamp or time.time()
        self.hash = self.calculate_hash()

    # Calculate the hash of the block using SHA-256
    def calculate_hash(self):
        block_data = f"{self.previous_hash}{self.transactions}{self.timestamp}".encode()
        return hashlib.sha256(block_data).hexdigest()

# Blockchain class to define the entire chain
class Blockchain:
    def __init__(self):
        self.chain = [self.create_genesis_block()]

    # Create the first block in the blockchain (Genesis block)
    def create_genesis_block(self):
        return Block("0", "Genesis Block")

    # Add a new block to the blockchain
    def add_block(self, transactions):
        previous_hash = self.chain[-1].hash
        new_block = Block(previous_hash, transactions)
        self.chain.append(new_block)
```

```
    # Verify the blockchain's integrity
    def is_chain_valid(self):
        for i in range(1, len(self.chain)):
            current_block = self.chain[i]
            previous_block = self.chain[i - 1]

            # Check if the current block's hash is correct
            if current_block.hash != current_block.calculate_hash():
                print(f"Block {i} has been tampered with.")
                return False

            # Check if the current block points correctly to the previous block
            if current_block.previous_hash != previous_block.hash:
                print(f"Block {i} has an invalid previous hash.")
                return False

        print("Blockchain is valid.")
        return True

    # Display the entire blockchain
    def display_chain(self):
        for i, block in enumerate(self.chain):
            print(f"Block {i}:")
            print(f"Previous Hash: {block.previous_hash}")
            print(f"Transactions: {block.transactions}")
            print(f"Timestamp: {time.ctime(block.timestamp)}")
            print(f"Hash: {block.hash}")
            print("-" * 30)

# Simulated transactions
transactions1 = "Alice sends 5 BTC to Bob"
transactions2 = "Bob sends 3 BTC to Charlie"
transactions3 = "Charlie sends 2 BTC to Dave"

# Initialize the blockchain
my_blockchain = Blockchain()

# Add new blocks with transactions
my_blockchain.add_block(transactions1)
my_blockchain.add_block(transactions2)
my_blockchain.add_block(transactions3)

# Display the blockchain
my_blockchain.display_chain()

# Check blockchain validity
my_blockchain.is_chain_valid()
```

Example output:

```
Block 0:
Previous Hash: 0
Transactions: Genesis Block
Timestamp: Thu Oct 19 13:41:25 2023
Hash: d93b1c47f82e1a837465e3c57f3cd0a86c28eebed80113ed129b761bf1f2540a
------------------------------
```

```
Block 1:
Previous Hash: d93b1c47f82e1a837465e3c57f3cd0a86c28eebed80113ed129b761bf1f2540a
Transactions: Alice sends 5 BTC to Bob
Timestamp: Thu Oct 19 13:41:25 2023
Hash: ecd214c6ae196ad6cf248cc6a40bcf41ad46aaecdf4a231b4a4e1f1f90cf9a15
------------------------------
Block 2:
Previous Hash: ecd214c6ae196ad6cf248cc6a40bcf41ad46aaecdf4a231b4a4e1f1f90cf9a15
Transactions: Bob sends 3 BTC to Charlie
Timestamp: Thu Oct 19 13:41:25 2023
Hash: 7f9b5e03e3bdbb63d465e745fe7e258ec82b658b34a74038e3705e848207376b
------------------------------
Block 3:
Previous Hash: 7f9b5e03e3bdbb63d465e745fe7e258ec82b658b34a74038e3705e848207376b
Transactions: Charlie sends 2 BTC to Dave
Timestamp: Thu Oct 19 13:41:25 2023
Hash: 95175a775660c172392f14f77df362e7fcbe69a48172f0e2ac8f9c4e5f00c194
------------------------------
Blockchain is valid.
```

Code Explanation:

Block Class: Each block contains:
- previous_hash: The hash of the previous block, ensuring the chain is linked.
- transactions: The list of transactions to be recorded.
- timestamp: The time the block is created.
- hash: The block's own hash, generated using SHA-256.

Blockchain Class:
- Genesis Block: The first block in the chain, with no previous hash.
- add_block(): A method to add new blocks to the chain.
- is_chain_valid(): A method to verify the integrity of the blockchain by checking whether each block's hash and previous hash are valid.
- display_chain(): A method to display the blocks and their contents (transactions, hashes, etc.).

Adding Transactions: Simulated transactions are added to the blockchain. Each new block contains a transaction and is linked to the previous block via its hash.

Blockchain Validation: The code checks whether the blockchain is valid by ensuring:
- Each block's hash matches the recalculated hash.
- Each block points correctly to the previous block.

Results:
- The blockchain was successfully created with three blocks, each containing transactions.
- The system verifies that the blockchain is valid by ensuring the hashes and previous hashes are consistent across all blocks, showcasing data integrity.
- Immutability is demonstrated as modifying any block would require altering all subsequent blocks, making it computationally infeasible without detection.

Benefits:

- Cybersecurity Application: This code demonstrates how blockchain technology can enhance security by ensuring that records, once added, cannot be tampered with. This is particularly important in sectors like finance, healthcare, and supply chain management, where data integrity is paramount.
- Decentralized Identity and Secure Data Sharing: Blockchain's decentralized nature, demonstrated in this code, also forms the basis for secure identity management and data-sharing solutions, reducing reliance on centralized authorities and minimizing attack surfaces.

Chapter 15

Emerging Technologies and Future Trends

Learning Outcomes:

Upon completing this chapter, you will be able to:

- *Explore the applications of AI and machine learning in cybersecurity, including threat detection, behavioral analysis, automated response, and adversarial AI.*
- *Understand the impact of quantum computing on cryptography, including breaking encryption, post-quantum cryptography (PQC), and quantum key distribution (QKD).*
- *Examine the applications of blockchain for security, including immutable ledgers, decentralized identity, and smart contracts, along with associated challenges.*
- *Analyze the security challenges posed by 5G networks, including increased attack surfaces, network slicing, authentication, and edge computing security.*
- *Discuss emerging threat landscapes such as AI-powered attacks, IoT vulnerabilities, supply chain attacks, and defense mechanisms including zero-trust architecture and collaborative defense.*

15.1 AI and Machine Learning in Cybersecurity

AI and machine learning (ML) have revolutionized cybersecurity by automating the detection of threats and enabling rapid responses. These technologies can analyze large amounts of data, recognize patterns, and identify anomalies, greatly reducing the time it takes to detect and mitigate cyber incidents.

Applications of AI and ML in Cybersecurity:

Threat Detection: Machine learning models can detect malware, phishing attempts, and denial-of-service attacks by identifying patterns in data. These models continuously learn from new data to enhance their accuracy.

Behavioral Analysis: AI-driven systems monitor user behavior, identifying deviations that may indicate compromised accounts or insider threats.

Automated Response: AI can automate responses to certain threats, such as isolating affected systems or blocking malicious traffic, enabling faster mitigation without requiring human intervention.

Adversarial AI: Cyber adversaries use AI to launch sophisticated attacks, such as bypassing machine learning defenses or tricking AI models. Defenses must evolve to protect against adversarial inputs.

Challenges:

Data Quality: AI models require high-quality data to be effective. In cybersecurity, data is often unstructured or incomplete, which can reduce model accuracy.

Adaptability: AI models must adapt to constantly evolving threats, requiring continuous retraining and updates.

Ethical Considerations: The use of AI in cybersecurity decision-making raises concerns around transparency, biases, and accountability.

15.2 Quantum Computing and Its Impact on Cryptography

Quantum computing presents both opportunities and challenges for cybersecurity. While quantum computers can solve complex problems quickly, they also threaten current cryptographic methods, necessitating the development of quantum-resistant alternatives.

Impact on Cryptography:

Breaking Encryption: Quantum computers could break widely used encryption methods, such as RSA and ECC, which rely on solving mathematically complex problems.

Post-Quantum Cryptography (PQC): Researchers are developing encryption algorithms that can withstand quantum attacks, ensuring secure communications in the quantum computing era.

Quantum Key Distribution (QKD): QKD uses quantum mechanics to securely distribute encryption keys. Any attempt to intercept these keys alters their state, making tampering easily detectable.

Challenges:

Timeline: While quantum computing is advancing, it is uncertain when quantum computers will become powerful enough to break current encryption methods.

Transition Period: Moving from traditional encryption to quantum-resistant encryption will require significant updates to software, hardware, and communication protocols.

Security Assurance: Ensuring the security of post-quantum cryptographic algorithms against both classical and quantum threats is essential.

15.3 Blockchain for Security

Blockchain technology offers decentralized, tamper-resistant systems that can enhance cybersecurity by ensuring data integrity, secure identity management, and transparent transactions.

Applications:

Immutable Ledger: Blockchain's immutable ledger ensures that recorded data cannot be altered, enhancing the security of financial transactions, audit trails, and sensitive data.

Decentralized Identity: Blockchain enables decentralized identity management, giving users control over their digital identities and reducing the risk of centralized breaches.

Smart Contracts: These are self-executing contracts embedded on the blockchain, automatically enforcing agreements and security protocols.

Challenges:

Scalability: Public blockchain networks face challenges in handling high transaction volumes, which may limit their adoption for large-scale security solutions.

Regulatory Compliance: The decentralized nature of blockchain complicates compliance with regulatory frameworks, particularly in privacy-sensitive industries like finance.

Privacy Concerns: While blockchain ensures transparency, it may conflict with privacy regulations like GDPR, which require data erasure and user control over personal information.

15.4 5G Security Challenges

The rollout of 5G networks introduces new security concerns due to their complexity and the sheer number of connected devices. While 5G promises faster speeds and greater connectivity, it also expands the attack surface for cybercriminals.

Key Challenges:

Increased Attack Surface: The massive number of connected IoT devices in 5G networks provides more entry points for attackers.

Network Slicing: 5G networks use network slicing to create virtual segments with different security requirements. Ensuring the security of each slice is critical to prevent cross-slice attacks.

Authentication and Authorization: The surge in connected devices calls for stronger mechanisms to prevent unauthorized access to 5G networks.

Edge Computing: 5G shifts data processing to the network's edge, increasing the need for robust security at distributed edge locations.

Security Measures:

Network Segmentation: Isolating critical infrastructure from non-essential network areas reduces the potential impact of security breaches.

Encryption: Encrypting data in transit across 5G networks helps prevent unauthorized access and data theft.

Continuous Monitoring: Real-time monitoring of 5G networks is essential for detecting and mitigating threats as they occur.

15.5 Future Threat Landscapes and Defense Mechanisms

As technology evolves, so do the threats facing organizations. AI-powered attacks, IoT vulnerabilities, and supply chain compromises are some of the key challenges cybersecurity professionals will face in the coming years.

Emerging Threats:

AI-Powered Attacks: Cyber adversaries are increasingly using AI to create more sophisticated malware, automate attacks, and evade detection.

IoT Vulnerabilities: The growing number of insecure IoT devices creates vulnerabilities that cybercriminals can exploit to launch large-scale attacks, such as DDoS attacks.

Supply Chain Attacks: Cyber attackers are targeting third-party vendors to infiltrate corporate networks, making supply chain security a critical focus.

Biometric Spoofing: Advances in deepfake technology pose risks to biometric authentication systems, which may be fooled by realistic spoofs.

Defense Mechanisms:

Zero Trust Architecture: This model assumes no implicit trust and continuously verifies the identity of users, devices, and applications before granting access.

AI-Driven Security Operations: AI-driven systems can automate much of the incident detection, triage, and response process, freeing human analysts to focus on more complex security issues.

Collaborative Defense: Sharing threat intelligence and best practices among industries and organizations can improve collective defenses against emerging cyber threats.

Quantum-Safe Cryptography: Organizations must invest in cryptographic solutions that can withstand both classical and quantum computing threats.

15.6 Summary

This chapter explored the impact of emerging technologies such as AI, quantum computing, blockchain, and 5G on cybersecurity, along with the challenges posed by future threats like AI-powered attacks and IoT vulnerabilities. Organizations must stay ahead by adopting advanced defense mechanisms, including zero-trust architecture, quantum-safe cryptography, and collaborative defense strategies, to prepare for the rapidly evolving cybersecurity landscape.

Exercise 15

1. Evaluate AI's Role in Cybersecurity: How could AI and machine learning improve your organization's cybersecurity strategy? What tools would you implement?

2. Post-Quantum Cryptography: Research the latest developments in quantum-safe cryptography and assess your organization's readiness for quantum computing threats.

3. Blockchain for Identity Management: Develop a plan for integrating blockchain into your organization's identity management system. Address scalability and privacy concerns.

4. 5G Security Plan: Design a security plan for a 5G network, focusing on network segmentation, edge computing, and IoT device security.

5. Collaborative Defense Strategy: Propose a strategy for collaborative defense in your industry, emphasizing how threat intelligence sharing can improve cybersecurity readiness.

Example Python Code for AI and Machine Learning Applications for Threat Detection

Context:

This Python example demonstrates how a basic machine learning model can classify network traffic as benign (safe) or malicious (potential threat). By leveraging machine learning, this approach automates threat detection, enabling quicker and more accurate identification of security breaches. This kind of automated detection is essential in managing high volumes of network data, as it helps to recognize patterns and anomalies that may otherwise go unnoticed.

Usefulness:

- Automated Threat Detection: Enhances the ability to detect potential threats in real time, reducing reliance on manual monitoring.
- Pattern Recognition: Identifies suspicious patterns in network traffic that may indicate malicious activity, helping to prevent breaches.
- Scalability: Suitable for high-traffic environments, making it feasible to monitor network activity at scale.

Input Features:

- Source IP Address: Identifies the origin of the network traffic.
- Destination IP Address: Specifies the target of the traffic, helping in tracking the flow of data.
- Protocol: The protocol used for communication (e.g., TCP, UDP), as certain attacks may exploit specific protocols.
- Packet Size: Size of the network packet, with unusually large or small packets potentially indicating malicious intent.
- Flags: Network flags (e.g., SYN, ACK) that can signal certain types of attacks based on packet behavior.

Code:

```
import pandas as pd
from sklearn.model_selection import train_test_split
from sklearn.ensemble import RandomForestClassifier
from sklearn.metrics import accuracy_score, classification_report

# Simulated network traffic dataset (could be replaced with real traffic data)
data = {
    'source_ip': ['192.168.1.1', '10.0.0.1', '192.168.1.2', '192.168.1.3', '10.0.0.2'],
    'dest_ip': ['192.168.1.100', '192.168.1.100', '10.0.0.2', '192.168.1.200', '10.0.0.3'],
    'protocol': [6, 17, 6, 6, 17],  # 6 = TCP, 17 = UDP
    'packet_size': [40, 1500, 60, 52, 1500],
    'flags': [0, 0, 2, 18, 0],  # SYN = 2, ACK = 16, SYN-ACK = 18
    'is_malicious': [0, 1, 0, 0, 1]  # 0 = benign, 1 = malicious
}

# Create a DataFrame
df = pd.DataFrame(data)

# Convert categorical IP addresses to numerical (dummy encoding for simplicity)
df_encoded = pd.get_dummies(df, columns=['source_ip', 'dest_ip', 'protocol'])

# Split the dataset into features (X) and target (y)
X = df_encoded.drop('is_malicious', axis=1)
y = df_encoded['is_malicious']
```

```
# Split into training and testing datasets
X_train, X_test, y_train, y_test = train_test_split(X, y, test_size=0.2, random_state=42)

# Train a Random Forest Classifier
clf = RandomForestClassifier(n_estimators=100, random_state=42)
clf.fit(X_train, y_train)

# Predict on the test set
y_pred = clf.predict(X_test)

# Evaluate the model
accuracy = accuracy_score(y_test, y_pred)
print(f"Accuracy: {accuracy:.4f}")

# Print classification report
print("Classification Report:")
print(classification_report(y_test, y_pred))
```

Example Output:

```
Accuracy: 1.0000
Classification Report:
              precision    recall  f1-score   support

           0       1.00      1.00      1.00         1
           1       1.00      1.00      1.00         1

    accuracy                           1.00         2
   macro avg       1.00      1.00      1.00         2
weighted avg       1.00      1.00      1.00         2
```

Code Explanation:

Dataset Creation: A simple dataset simulates network traffic with features such as source/destination IPs, protocol type, packet size, flags, and a label indicating if the traffic is benign (0) or malicious (1).

Data Preprocessing: One-hot encoding is used to convert categorical IP addresses and protocol types into numeric features, suitable for machine learning.

Splitting Data: The data is split into training (80%) and testing (20%) sets using `train_test_split()` from Scikit-learn.

Model Training: A Random Forest Classifier, an ensemble learning method, is used to train on the network traffic data to distinguish between benign and malicious traffic.

Prediction and Evaluation: The model predicts on the test set and evaluates performance using accuracy and a classification report (precision, recall, F1-score).

Key Concepts Demonstrated:

- AI and Machine Learning in Cybersecurity: The Random Forest model learns patterns in the network traffic data to detect whether a given packet is benign or malicious. This can help automate threat detection.

- Behavioral Analysis: The system analyzes features such as packet size, protocol, and flags to detect anomalies in network traffic, indicative of potential Advanced Persistent Threats (APTs).

- Automated Response: Once a malicious packet is detected, an organization could implement automated responses such as blocking traffic or isolating compromised systems in a real-world application.

Benefits:

- Cybersecurity Application: This code demonstrates a practical example of machine learning in cybersecurity. It shows how AI can detect threats in network traffic by analyzing patterns and behavior, which can enhance the effectiveness of incident response plans.

- Proactive Measures: Organizations can use similar machine learning techniques to build systems that monitor network traffic in real time, flag potential threats, and trigger defensive actions automatically.

Chapter 16

Legal and Ethical Considerations in Cybersecurity

Learning Outcomes:

Upon completing this chapter, you will be able to:

- *Understand key cybersecurity laws and regulations, including GDPR, HIPAA, and CCPA, and their implications for data protection and compliance.*
- *Explore the role of ethical hacking and penetration testing in identifying vulnerabilities and improving cybersecurity defenses.*
- *Learn about responsible disclosure practices and vulnerability management to enhance organizational security.*
- *Discuss the legal implications of cyber incidents, including data breach notification requirements, forensic investigations, and liability.*
- *Examine regulatory compliance challenges, industry-specific regulations, and international laws affecting cybersecurity practices.*

16.1 Cybersecurity Laws and Regulations

In today's digital environment, organizations face an array of complex cybersecurity laws that govern the collection, storage, and processing of personal data. Compliance with these regulations is crucial to avoid legal consequences and protect individuals' privacy.

Key Regulations:

GDPR (General Data Protection Regulation): Applicable across the European Union, GDPR regulates the processing of personal data and emphasizes data subjects' rights, transparency, and accountability. It requires businesses to implement data protection measures, obtain explicit consent, and report data breaches within 72 hours.

HIPAA (Health Insurance Portability and Accountability Act): In the U.S., HIPAA mandates the protection of patient health information (PHI) through administrative, physical, and technical safeguards. It applies to healthcare providers, insurers, and business associates handling PHI.

CCPA (California Consumer Privacy Act): CCPA grants California residents the right to know, access, delete, and opt out of the sale of their personal data. It requires businesses to be transparent about their data collection practices and imposes penalties for violations.

Key Aspects of Cybersecurity Laws:

Data Breach Notification: Many regulations require prompt notification of affected individuals and authorities in the event of a data breach. The notification should detail the extent of the breach and the steps being taken to mitigate its impact.

Data Protection Principles: Regulations emphasize securing personal data through encryption, access controls, and continuous monitoring to ensure lawful processing and minimize risks.

Compliance and Penalties: Non-compliance can result in significant fines. For example, GDPR fines can be as high as €20 million or 4% of global revenue, whichever is greater.

16.2 Ethical Hacking and Penetration Testing

To enhance security defenses, organizations often employ ethical hackers and conduct penetration tests to simulate attacks and identify vulnerabilities before malicious actors exploit them.

Ethical Hacking:
Purpose: Ethical hackers are authorized to attempt to breach an organization's systems in a controlled manner, identifying security weaknesses that could be exploited by cybercriminals.

Scope: Ethical hackers must work within defined parameters and follow legal guidelines to avoid disrupting business operations.

Methodology: Ethical hackers use techniques similar to real-world attackers, such as social engineering, vulnerability scanning, and exploiting known vulnerabilities.

Penetration Testing:
Purpose: Penetration testing simulates cyber-attacks to assess the effectiveness of an organization's security controls and uncover weaknesses in systems, networks, or applications.

Types of Testing:
- External Testing: Focuses on external-facing assets, such as websites and servers.
- Internal Testing: Simulates attacks from within the organization, including insider threats.

Benefits: Penetration testing provides organizations with actionable insights to strengthen security and address vulnerabilities before they are exploited.

16.3 Responsible Disclosure and Vulnerability Management

Vulnerability management and responsible disclosure are critical components of maintaining a secure cybersecurity posture, ensuring that security flaws are addressed responsibly.

Responsible Disclosure:
Definition: Responsible disclosure involves reporting vulnerabilities to the affected organization in a way that allows them time to fix the issue before publicizing it.

Process: Researchers provide detailed reports, including proof-of-concept attacks, and offer remediation advice while giving organizations time to patch vulnerabilities before releasing public information.

Benefits: This practice fosters collaboration between security researchers and organizations, minimizing the risk of exploitation by malicious actors.

Vulnerability Management:
Lifecycle: Effective vulnerability management involves continuously scanning systems, identifying risks, prioritizing vulnerabilities, and applying fixes.

Tools: Organizations often use automated tools, such as Nessus or Qualys, to detect and manage vulnerabilities across their networks.

Patch Management: Regularly applying software patches and updates helps mitigate known vulnerabilities and reduces the attack surface.

16.4 Legal Implications of Cyber Incidents

Cyber incidents can result in significant legal consequences for organizations, particularly regarding data breaches and cybersecurity compliance. Organizations must be aware of their legal obligations and ensure they follow best practices for handling cyber incidents.

Key Legal Considerations:

Data Breach Notification: Regulations like GDPR and CCPA require organizations to notify affected individuals and authorities promptly after a breach. Failure to do so can result in penalties and reputational damage.

Forensic Investigation: After a cyber incident, organizations must conduct forensic investigations to understand the scope and cause of the breach. These investigations are vital for regulatory compliance, insurance claims, and assessing legal liability.

Liability: If negligence is proven—such as a failure to implement appropriate security measures—organizations can be held legally liable for damages caused by a data breach or security incident.

Regulatory Compliance:

Industry-Specific Regulations: Certain sectors, such as healthcare (HIPAA), finance (PCI-DSS), and government, have specific cybersecurity requirements. Organizations in these sectors must adhere to strict compliance guidelines.

International Laws: Global organizations must navigate different laws across jurisdictions, particularly in managing cross-border data transfers and complying with country-specific cybersecurity regulations.

Legal Protections for Security Researchers:

Safe Harbor: Some jurisdictions provide legal protections to security researchers who conduct authorized vulnerability testing in good faith, ensuring they are not penalized for responsible disclosure.

Bug Bounty Programs: Many organizations offer bug bounty programs that provide financial rewards for researchers who discover and responsibly disclose security vulnerabilities.

16.5 Summary

This chapter examined the legal and ethical considerations in cybersecurity, including the regulatory landscape, ethical hacking practices, responsible disclosure, and the legal implications of cyber incidents. Organizations must stay compliant with laws like GDPR, HIPAA, and CCPA while employing ethical hacking and vulnerability management to protect their data and systems. By understanding the legal implications of cyber incidents and regulatory requirements, organizations can mitigate risks and strengthen their cybersecurity strategies.

Exercise 16

1. Compliance Assessment:
   - Assess your organization's compliance with GDPR, HIPAA, or other relevant data protection laws. Identify any gaps and develop a plan to address them.

2. Penetration Testing Plan:
   - Develop a penetration testing plan for your organization. Define the scope, objectives, and reporting structure for testing your organization's cybersecurity defenses.

3. Vulnerability Management Strategy:
   - Create a vulnerability management strategy, including the use of scanning tools, prioritization techniques, and patch management to mitigate risks.

4. Incident Response Plan:
   - Draft an incident response plan that outlines legal obligations for breach notification, forensic investigation procedures, and communication strategies.

5. International Compliance:
   - Research the international cybersecurity laws applicable to your organization. Propose strategies for achieving compliance across different jurisdictions, focusing on cross-border data transfers and regulatory differences.

Example Python Code for Vulnerability Management

Context:

This Python example utilizes the Nmap tool to conduct a basic scan on a specified IP address, identifying open ports and services. This type of scanning simulates the process of ethical hacking or penetration testing, helping cybersecurity professionals detect potential vulnerabilities in a network. Once identified, these vulnerabilities can be reported and addressed as part of a comprehensive vulnerability management strategy.

Usefulness:

- Vulnerability Detection: Quickly identifies open ports and running services, which could be potential entry points for attackers.
- Penetration Testing: Provides insights into system weaknesses that can be remediated to strengthen security.
- Network Inventory: Offers an overview of active services and ports, aiding in network management and monitoring.

Input Features:

- Target IP: Specifies the IP address or range to be scanned for open ports and active services.
- Scan Type: Defines the type of scan (e.g., SYN scan, service scan) to determine the nature of open ports and the status of services.
- Port Range: Sets the range of ports to scan, focusing on those most likely to expose vulnerabilities.

Code:

```
import nmap

# Function to scan the target for open ports and services
def scan_target(target_ip, port_range="1-1024"):
    # Initialize the nmap scanner object
    nm = nmap.PortScanner()

    print(f"Starting scan on {target_ip} for ports {port_range}")

    # Perform a scan on the target IP and specified port range
    nm.scan(target_ip, port_range, arguments='-sV')

    # Display the scan results
    for host in nm.all_hosts():
        print(f"\nHost: {host} ({nm[host].hostname()})")
        print(f"State: {nm[host].state()}")

        for proto in nm[host].all_protocols():
            print(f"Protocol: {proto}")

            ports = nm[host][proto].keys()
            for port in ports:
                print(f"Port:  {port},  State:  {nm[host][proto][port]['state']},  Service:
{nm[host][proto][port]['name']}")

# Define the target IP address (this can be changed as needed)
target_ip = "192.168.1.1"  # Example IP address
```

```
# Perform the scan
scan_target(target_ip)
--------------------------------------------------------------------------------

Example Output:
Starting scan on 192.168.1.1 for ports 1-1024

Host: 192.168.1.1 ()
State: up
Protocol: tcp
Port: 80, State: open, Service: http
Port: 22, State: open, Service: ssh
Port: 443, State: open, Service: https
```

Code Explanation:

nmap Module:

The script uses the nmap module to perform a scan of a given target IP. The nmap tool is widely used for network discovery and vulnerability scanning by both ethical hackers and security analysts.

scan_target Function:

- This function accepts a target IP and an optional port range to scan.
- The `nmap.PortScanner()` object is initialized to start the scanning process.
- The scan is performed using the `-sV` argument to detect open ports and services running on the system.

Scan Results:

- The script prints out the status of the target host, including its open ports, the state of those ports (open or closed), and the services associated with those ports (e.g., HTTP, FTP).
- This helps security professionals identify potentially vulnerable services that may need to be patched or mitigated.

Ethical Hacking and Penetration Testing:

- This example simulates part of a penetration test where a network or system is scanned for open ports and services.
- The identified vulnerabilities can be reported following responsible disclosure practices, ensuring that they are remediated in a controlled and secure manner.

Key Concepts Demonstrated:

Vulnerability Management: This script scans for open ports and services, helping security teams identify potential vulnerabilities (e.g., outdated software or misconfigured services). These vulnerabilities can then be patched or mitigated as part of a larger vulnerability management process.

Ethical Hacking and Penetration Testing: The scan simulates a penetration test where an ethical hacker tries to find weaknesses in a network's perimeter. Identified weaknesses can then be communicated to the organization using responsible disclosure practices.

Legal and Ethical Considerations:
- Ethical hacking activities should always be conducted with proper authorization and under defined rules of engagement.
- Identified vulnerabilities should be disclosed responsibly, giving the organization time to fix them before making the information public.
- Conducting unauthorized scans on external systems could lead to legal consequences, which is why adherence to cybersecurity laws and regulations is crucial.

Data Protection Laws: The results from this type of scanning can help organizations comply with regulations such as GDPR and HIPAA by identifying weak points in network security that could lead to unauthorized data access or breaches.

Benefits:
- Regulatory Compliance: Running regular scans and patching vulnerabilities helps organizations stay compliant with cybersecurity regulations like GDPR and HIPAA, which require a high level of security for data protection.
- Proactive Defense: This tool helps detect potential attack vectors before they are exploited by malicious actors, which is essential for maintaining a strong cybersecurity posture.

Appendix A: Cybersecurity Tools – Functions and Usage

A.1 Introduction

Cybersecurity tools play a crucial role in defending systems, networks, and applications against ever-evolving threats. These tools assist cybersecurity professionals in detecting, preventing, analyzing, and responding to cyberattacks. This appendix introduces essential categories of cybersecurity tools, their core functions, and practical examples widely used in the industry.

A.2 Categories of Cybersecurity Tools and Examples

Network Monitoring and Packet Analysis Tools:

Purpose: Capture, inspect, and analyze network traffic for anomalies or signs of malicious activities.

Tool	Function	Example Use
Wireshark	Network packet capture and deep analysis	Analyze suspicious network traffic
tcpdump	Command-line packet capture	Monitor packets from a specific IP or port
SolarWinds Network Performance Monitor	Real-time network monitoring	Detect unusual bandwidth spikes

Vulnerability Assessment and Scanning Tools:

Purpose: Identify known vulnerabilities in systems, applications, and networks.

Tool	Function	Example Use
Nessus	Vulnerability scanner	Detect outdated software or missing patches
OpenVAS	Open-source vulnerability assessment	Scan internal networks for CVEs
Nikto	Web server vulnerability scanning	Identify misconfigurations and outdated server software

Penetration Testing and Exploitation Tools:

Purpose: Simulate cyberattacks to find exploitable vulnerabilities.

Tool	Function	Example Use
Metasploit Framework	Exploitation and payload delivery	Test exploitability of system vulnerabilities
Burp Suite	Web application penetration testing	Detect SQL injection or XSS vulnerabilities
John the Ripper	Password cracking	Test password strength

Endpoint Protection and Malware Analysis Tools:

Purpose: Detect, prevent, and analyze malware threats on endpoint devices.

Tool	Function	Example Use
Microsoft Defender for Endpoint	Endpoint detection and response (EDR)	Detect ransomware activity
YARA	Malware pattern matching	Identify malware in files or memory
Cuckoo Sandbox	Automated malware analysis	Observe malware behavior in a safe environment

Security Information and Event Management (SIEM) Tools:

Purpose: Aggregate, analyze, and correlate log data for detecting threats.

Tool	Function	Example Use
Splunk	Log analysis and threat detection	Detect brute force login attempts
ELK Stack (Elasticsearch, Logstash, Kibana)	Open-source SIEM for visualization and analysis	Correlate events from multiple sources
IBM QRadar	Advanced threat detection and incident response	Monitor large enterprise environments

Firewall and Intrusion Detection/Prevention Systems (IDS/IPS):

Purpose: Monitor and control incoming/outgoing network traffic based on rules.

Tool	**Function**	**Example Use**
Snort	Open-source IDS/IPS	Detect port scan or brute-force attempts
Suricata	IDS/IPS with multi-threading	Monitor high-speed network traffic
pfSense	Firewall and routing platform	Protect small business or home networks

Threat Intelligence Platforms and Forensics Tools:

Purpose: Collect and analyze threat data; conduct digital forensics.

Tool	**Function**	**Example Use**
MISP	Threat intelligence sharing platform	Share malware hashes and indicators
Autopsy	Digital forensics platform	Recover deleted files during an investigation
FTK (Forensic Toolkit)	Comprehensive forensic analysis	Analyze disk images and memory dumps

A.3 Common Tool Functions Summary

Function	Example Tools
Network Traffic Analysis	Wireshark, tcpdump
Vulnerability Scanning	Nessus, OpenVAS
Penetration Testing	Metasploit, Burp Suite
Endpoint Protection/EDR	Microsoft Defender, Carbon Black
Malware Detection & Analysis	YARA, Cuckoo Sandbox
Log Management & SIEM	Splunk, ELK Stack
Firewall/IDS/IPS	Snort, Suricata, pfSense
Digital Forensics & Incident Response	Autopsy, FTK
Threat Intelligence	MISP, OpenCTI

A.4 Sample Command Example (Wireshark/tcpdump/YARA)

Example: Running a simple tcpdump capture

sudo tcpdump -i eth0 -w capture.pcap

Purpose: Captures all traffic on interface eth0 and saves it for analysis.

Example: Using YARA to scan for malware patterns

yara malware_rules.yar suspect_file.exe

Purpose: Matches the suspect file against defined YARA malware rules.

A.5 Visual – Cybersecurity Tools Grouped by Function

CYBERSECURITY FUNCTION	EXAMPLE TOOLS
Network Analysis	Wireshark, tcpdump
Vulnerability Scanning	Nessus, OpenVAS, Nikto
Penetration Testing	Metasploit, Burp Suite, John the Ripper
Endpoint Protection & Malware Analysis	Defender, YARA, Cuckoo
SIEM & Log Analysis	Splunk, ELK, QRadar
Firewall / IDS / IPS	Snort, Suricata, pfSense
Forensics & Threat Intelligence	MISP, Autopsy, FTK

A.6 Summary

Cybersecurity professionals rely on a wide range of tools for defense, detection, testing, and investigation. This appendix introduced essential tools across various cybersecurity domains—network security, endpoint protection, malware analysis, threat intelligence, and digital forensics. Mastering these tools enhances a professional's ability to protect systems, investigate incidents, and mitigate risks effectively.

Appendix B: MITRE ATT&CK Framework – Purpose and Application

B.1 Introduction to MITRE ATT&CK

The MITRE ATT&CK® Framework (Adversarial Tactics, Techniques, and Common Knowledge) is a globally accessible knowledge base that systematically documents the behavior of real-world adversaries.

- Purpose: Help organizations understand how attackers operate after gaining access to a system or network.
- Focus: Maps Tactics (goals), Techniques (how goals are achieved), and Procedures (specific implementations) of known cyber threats.

Originally developed by MITRE Corporation for defensive cybersecurity teams, ATT&CK is widely used for Threat Modelling:

- Defensive gap analysis
- Detection development
- Red and blue team exercises

B.2 Components of the Framework

Component	Description	Example
Tactics	The adversary's technical objectives during an attack.	Execution, Persistence, Exfiltration
Techniques	General methods adversaries use to achieve a tactic.	Scripting (T1059), Spear Phishing (T1566)
Sub-Techniques	Specific variations of techniques.	Scripting → PowerShell (T1059.001)
Procedures	Real-world examples of how specific groups implement techniques.	APT28 using Mimikatz for credential dumping

B.3 Example of Tactic → Technique → Procedure Mapping

Tactic	Technique (ID)	Example Procedure
Persistence	DLL Sideloading (T1574.002)	Attackers load malicious DLLs via trusted apps
Execution	PowerShell (T1059.001)	APT29 uses PowerShell scripts for data exfiltration
Credential Access	Credential Dumping (T1003)	Mimikatz used to extract credentials
Exfiltration	Exfiltration Over DNS (T1048.003)	DNS tunneling of stolen data

B.4 Use Cases of MITRE ATT&CK in Cybersecurity

1. Threat Detection and Defense Improvement

- Map detected alerts or incidents to known techniques.
- Identify detection gaps in your SOC or SIEM coverage.

2. Red Teaming / Adversary Simulation

- Design red team exercises based on real-world techniques.
- Measure how well blue teams detect simulated adversary behavior.

3. Threat Intelligence Integration

- Connect threat intel reports to known ATT&CK techniques.
- Track which APT groups use specific tactics.

4. Incident Response and Forensics

- Use ATT&CK mapping during post-incident analysis to reconstruct attack chains.

B.5 Example: Using ATT&CK for Detection Planning

MITRE Tactic	Technique	Detection Example
Execution	T1059 - Command and Scripting Interpreter	Monitor PowerShell logs (Event ID 4104)
Credential Access	T1003 - LSASS Memory Dump	Detect access to lsass.exe memory
Lateral Movement	T1021 - Remote Services (RDP)	Monitor unusual RDP connections

B.6 Online Resources

- Official MITRE ATT&CK site: https://attack.mitre.org
- Enterprise Matrix: Techniques mapped to enterprise environments.
- Cloud and ICS Matrices: Specialized matrices for cloud and industrial systems.

B.7 Sample MITRE ATT&CK Flow Tactic to Technique Mapping

Tactic: Initial Access — Technique: Phishing (T1566)

Tactic: Execution — Technique: PowerShell (T1059.001)

Tactic: Persistence — Technique: Scheduled Task (T1053)

Tactic: Credential Access — Technique: LSASS Dump (T1003)

Tactic: Exfiltration — Technique: DNS Tunneling (T1048.003)

B.8 Summary

The MITRE ATT&CK framework is a vital tool for cybersecurity practitioners to understand adversary behavior, improve detection strategies, and prioritize defenses based on real-world attack techniques. Its structured knowledge base empowers organizations to simulate, detect, respond to, and learn from cyber threats effectively.

Appendix C: Windows OS Commands Relevant to Cybersecurity

C.1 Introduction

Cybersecurity analysts frequently use Windows native commands for incident investigation, threat hunting, system monitoring, and forensics. PowerShell adds additional capability for automation and deep system interrogation.

This appendix lists essential Windows CMD and PowerShell commands, their functions, and practical use cases in cybersecurity.

C.2 Essential CMD Commands for Cybersecurity Tasks

Command	Function / Usage	Example
ipconfig /all	Display full network configuration	View IP, DNS, MAC addresses
netstat -ano	Show active network connections and listening ports	Identify suspicious connections (with PID)
tasklist	List all running processes	Identify unknown/malicious processes
taskkill /PID <pid> /F	Terminate process by PID	Kill malicious or suspicious process
systeminfo	Display OS version, patches, system uptime	Check patch levels and system vulnerabilities
net user	List all local user accounts	Detect unauthorized user creation
net localgroup administrators	List admin group members	Spot privilege escalation
dir /s /b <filename>	Search entire drive for a file	Find dropped malware or suspicious scripts
fc /b file1 file2	Compare two files in binary mode	Check for file tampering
whoami /priv	Show current user's privileges	Check if running as admin
wmic process list full	List running processes with full details	Analyze process tree
sc query	List running services	Spot suspicious or unknown services
netsh advfirewall show allprofiles	Display Windows Firewall status	Check firewall rules and state

C.3 Essential PowerShell Commands for Security Monitoring

PowerShell Command	Purpose / Example Use
Get-Process	List running processes with CPU and memory usage
Get-Service	Display status of all Windows services
Get-EventLog -LogName Security -Newest 20	Retrieve latest security events
Get-WmiObject Win32_NetworkAdapterConfiguration	View network configuration and MAC addresses
Get-LocalUser	List all local users
Get-LocalGroupMember -Group "Administrators"	Identify who has administrative privileges
Get-ScheduledTask	List all scheduled tasks
Get-ChildItem -Recurse -Filter "*.ps1"	Search system for PowerShell scripts
Get-Content -Path <file>	Read content of a suspicious file or script
Set-ExecutionPolicy Restricted	Block PowerShell script execution
Invoke-WebRequest <url>	Test external connectivity or check C2 communications
Get-WinEvent -LogName Microsoft-Windows-Sysmon/Operational	View Sysmon logs for deeper process and network event tracing

C.4 Example Use Cases in Cybersecurity Operations

Use Case	Command	Purpose
Detect active C2 connections	netstat -ano	Identify external suspicious connections
Check persistence mechanisms	Get-ScheduledTask / schtasks /query /fo LIST	Look for unauthorized or hidden scheduled tasks
Find suspicious PowerShell use	Get-WinEvent -LogName PowerShell -MaxEvents 50	Detect potentially malicious PowerShell executions
Privilege escalation check	net localgroup administrators	Look for unauthorized admin user additions
Malware hunting - find scripts	Get-ChildItem -Path C:\ -Recurse -Filter "*.vbs"	Locate VBScript files that could be part of malware
Extract event logs	wevtutil epl Security C:\logs\security.evtx	Export Windows Event Logs for forensic analysis

C.5 Windows Forensics & Incident Response Tips

Registry Check:
reg query HKLM\Software\Microsoft\Windows\CurrentVersion\Run
- View autorun entries (often used by malware for persistence)

Memory Dump Collection:
tasklist + procdump
- Capture process memory for malware analysis

Prefetch Analysis:
dir C:\Windows\Prefetch\
- See programs recently executed (useful in forensic timeline)

C.6 Cybersecurity Tools Grouped By Function

CYBERSECURITY TASK CATEGORY	COMMON WINDOWS COMMANDS
Network Monitoring	netstat -ano ipconfig /all Get-WmiObject Win32_NetworkAdapterConfiguration
Process & Service Monitoring	tasklist taskkill /PID <pid> Get-Process Get-Service
User & Privilege Checks	net user whoami /priv Get-LocalUser Get-LocalGroupMember -Group 'Administrators'
File & Script Hunting	*dir /s /b .ps1 **Get-ChildItem -Recurse -Filter ".vbs"*** Get-Content <file>
Scheduled Tasks & Persistence	schtasks /query Get-ScheduledTask reg query HKLM...\Run
Event Logs & Forensics	Get-EventLog -LogName Security wevtutil epl security Get-WinEvent -LogName PowerShell

C.7 Summary

Mastering Windows native commands and PowerShell is crucial for cybersecurity tasks such as **incident response**, **threat hunting**, **forensics**, and **system hardening**. These commands provide deep visibility into the system's behavior, allowing analysts to detect and investigate malicious activities effectively.

Appendix D: Linux Commands for Cybersecurity Tasks

D.1 Introduction

Linux systems are widely used in servers, cloud infrastructure, and cybersecurity labs. Mastery of Linux command-line tools is crucial for penetration testing, incident response, threat hunting, and system hardening.

This appendix covers essential Linux commands, options, and practical use cases for cybersecurity.

D.2 Network Monitoring and Analysis

Command	Function / Use
ifconfig / ip addr	Display network interfaces and IP addresses
netstat -tulpn	Show active connections and listening ports
ss -tuln	Replacement for netstat with more detailed socket info
tcpdump -i eth0	Capture network packets on interface eth0
nmap -sS <target>	Perform TCP SYN scan on target host
wireshark	GUI tool for packet capture and analysis
dig <domain>	DNS query investigation

D.3 File System, Process, and Privilege Checks

Command	Function / Use
ls -la	List files/directories with detailed permissions
find / -name "malware.sh"	Search entire system for suspicious file
grep -i "password" /etc/passwd	Search for keyword "password" inside files
ps aux	List running processes with user and CPU/mem usage
top or htop	Monitor processes interactively
whoami	Show current user
sudo -l	Show commands user can run as root
`history	grep wget`

D.4 User, Group, and Permission Monitoring

Command	Function / Use
cat /etc/passwd	List user accounts
cat /etc/group	List groups
id <username>	Show user and group IDs
chmod 700 <file>	Set strict permissions on sensitive files
chown user:group <file>	Change file ownership

D.5 System and Kernel Info Collection

Command	Function / Use
uname -a	Display kernel version and system architecture
df -h	Show disk space usage
uptime	Check system running time
`dmesg	less`
last	View login history

D.6 Malware and Rootkit Scanning Tools (Linux CLI)

Tool / Command	Purpose
chkrootkit	Scan for known rootkits
rkhunter --check	Check for rootkits, backdoors, and local exploits
clamscan -r /home	Scan directory recursively for viruses
file suspicious.bin	Identify file types
`strings suspicious.bin	less`

D.7 Log Analysis and Incident Investigation

Command	Function / Use
cat /var/log/auth.log	Review authentication logs
grep "Failed password" /var/log/auth.log	Detect failed SSH login attempts
journalctl -xe	Analyze system logs with journalctl
tail -f /var/log/syslog	Monitor system log in real time
awk '{print $1,$2,$3}' /var/log/syslog	Extract specific fields from logs

D.8 Example Linux Forensic Commands

Check open files by process:

lsof -p <PID>

Find hidden files and directories:

find / -name ".*" -type f

Check file hash for integrity validation:

sha256sum suspicious_file

D.9 Linux Cybersecurity Command Cheat Sheet

CYBERSECURITY TASK CATEGORY	COMMON LINUX COMMANDS
Network Monitoring & Scanning	ifconfig, netstat, tcpdump, nmap, wireshark, dig
Process & File Analysis	ls -la, find, grep, ps aux, top, strings
User, Group & Permission Checks	cat /etc/passwd, chmod, chown, id, sudo -l
System & Kernel Info	uname -a, df -h, uptime, dmesg, last
Malware & Rootkit Scanning	chkrootkit, rkhunter, clamscan, file
Log Analysis & Forensics	cat /var/log/auth.log, journalctl, tail -f, awk

D.10 Summary

Linux provides a rich command-line environment essential for cybersecurity practitioners. From monitoring and analysis to malware detection and forensics, these commands offer direct access to system internals.

Understanding and practicing these commands improves the ability to detect, investigate, and respond to cyber incidents in Linux environments.

www.ingramcontent.com/pod-product-compliance
Ingram Content Group UK Ltd.
Pitfield, Milton Keynes, MK11 3LW, UK
UKHW061134310726
14090UKWH00038B/1443